T0330368

Management Control and Creativity

Smart Innovation Set

coordinated by
Dimitri Uzunidis

Volume 41

Management Control and Creativity

*Challenges of Managing
Innovation Processes*

Sophie Bollinger

WILEY

First published 2023 in Great Britain and the United States by ISTE Ltd and John Wiley & Sons, Inc.

ISTE Ltd
27-37 St George's Road
London SW19 4EU
UK

www.iste.co.uk

John Wiley & Sons, Inc.
111 River Street
Hoboken, NJ 07030
USA

www.wiley.com

Any opinions, findings, and conclusions or recommendations expressed in this material are those of the author(s), contributor(s) or editor(s) and do not necessarily reflect the views of ISTE Group.

Library of Congress Control Number: 2023940542

British Library Cataloguing-in-Publication Data
A CIP record for this book is available from the British Library
ISBN 978-1-78630-819-1

Contents

Foreword

We live in a period of rapid change where companies must innovate at an increasingly fast pace to differentiate themselves. However, these clichés no longer fully reflect the realities of today. While it is true that the speed of innovation and exploitation cycles have accelerated, the situation in which organizations find themselves differs from previous periods both structurally and cyclically:

– From a structural perspective, the methods for developing innovations have become more widespread, professionalized and open to others. As a result, organizations have begun to value the creativity of their employees more. New performance criteria are emerged, contrasting with older norms such as the ability to execute and develop innovation with the utmost secrecy. Innovation management, and more broadly change management, has adapted to a more volatile, uncertain, complex and ambiguous world.

– From a cyclic perspective, the COVID-19 pandemic came later than most of the work presented in this book, and it has given greater freedom of action to managers and teams in charge of producing innovations. Indeed, innovation was necessary, and organizations had to react quickly to changes in the environment and sudden shifts in demand. This newfound freedom has made it possible to take initiatives and risks, as the need to do so ignores the old routines.

Faced with this increase in creativity, possibilities and opportunities, some organizations are thinking about implementing new forms of control to limit abuse without curbing the creativity of employees.

The author proposes an exploration of the theories and tools available to managers to achieve this balance between rigor and creativity.

F.1. The environment, a structural and cyclical change

VUCA is a popular term in management that summarizes in one expression the situation a manager is confronted with. This acronym, which stands for "Volatility, Uncertainty, Complexity, Ambiguity", has become in some companies a synonym for "difficult to manage" or "chaotic".

The concept was introduced in 1987 in a military context to describe confusing situations, such as the end of the Cold War, which mixed political and military aspects. Since then, the term has spread to other domains that require leadership in challenging situations. The Cynefin model shares similarities with this approach and is discussed in the book *Pro en management* co-written by the author.

This acronym also captures the situation in which managers of innovative projects find themselves. They find themselves defending a project that needs time to materialize, in a changing environment, against other competing projects, and skeptical managers who question the changing needs of consumers. The work summarized in Chapters 1 and 2 presents innovation process management models that help managers to develop their understanding of these environmental changes.

F.2. Control, an omnipresent need in organizations

Henry Ford pushed the limits of control very far in his factories. In particular, he set up a specific control unit whose activity was to control the workers not only at work but also outside of it! Ford believed that workers who did not drink, gamble, or fight and led a normal family life worked better and were more productive. Thus, workers who lived an exemplary life received a better salary. This system did not satisfy the workers, who felt constantly watched and pressured. The balance between control and freedom, and between private and professional life, is still an issue. In an organization, control means checking whether everything is done by the adopted plan and the instructions that have been given. Monitoring is necessary to find out whether plans are being carried out according to what has been recommended and whether they are being executed properly. It also allows for the identification of deviations from the plan so that corrective actions can be taken. However, the control must be balanced. Chapter 3 is dedicated to the formal and informal methods of control that need to be combined in a clever way within each organization.

F.3. Being creative in a highly controlled environment?

IBM's control system has been widely copied by other companies. Most of IBM's success comes from a fairly rigid system and codes followed by the employees. Yet, when the company developed its first computer, engineers and scientists in the R&D unit were allowed to collaborate with people outside the company to obtain knowledge that was not held in-house. The very tight schedule that the company imposed on them required them to resort to solutions that already existed and had been invented by others. It was also a real reason to look for skills outside the company's borders in order to move as quickly as possible, but other arguments were often put forward. For example, creativity would not be possible within a very controlled environment, and that is why IBM allowed engineers to contact partners and temporarily leave the corporate environment. This is a way to give a group of employees more freedom without changing the dominant corporate culture or creating jealousy. However, the creative freedom of the engineers, the objectives of the leaders and the vision of the managers in charge of control are not always compatible. This problem is found in all organizations, regardless of the size of the company (SME or multinational), the sector of activity or the control tools used. In Chapter 4, Sophie Bollinger proposes to explore an often-neglected sector, the social and solidarity economy. In this sector, the notions of control and innovation are at the center of distinct tensions in the study and reveal problems and solutions that can inspire companies in all sectors.

F.4. What is the future for work on control, innovation and creativity?

In her work, Bollinger questions the "meaning" of innovation. In the background, she raises the question of the societal value of innovations. After bullshit jobs, are we seeing the development of bullshit innovations? Can the search for a better combination of creativity methods and control practices reduce the development and dissemination of these innovations, which are more harmful than truly value-creating in the long term? This reflection leads the author to study historical sectors that are far from the notion of an innovation process while being hostile to the concept of control. Thus, she studies non-profit organizations, whose practices she compares to those of more traditional economic activities.

F.5. A word about the author and her background

This book is the result of Bollinger's thesis work. Her course of study has allowed her to combine a remarkable academic career that has led her to become a teacher-researcher in the Faculty of Economics and Management at the University of Strasbourg. Her research is conducted at the BETA laboratory, UMR CNRS Inrae, in the fields of control applied to innovation and creativity in various organizational contexts.

BETA is a research laboratory that celebrated its 50th anniversary in 2022. The researchers in this laboratory distinguished themselves early on by their research approach, which combines economics and management sciences, theory and applied practice. They were among the first to work on the notions of communities, evolutionary economics and management or routines. In line with the researchers of this laboratory, Bollinger draws on principles established in several disciplines related to management, including economics, and more broadly the disciplines that have examined the notion of creativity, in order to provide rigorous work that is at the cutting edge of knowledge in the field and that is interested in the real practices of companies.

She teaches the results obtained from her work as well as innovation management and control in the Faculty of Economics and Management at the undergraduate and graduate levels, and to seasoned professionals in Master of Business Administration.

Thierry BURGER-HELMCHEN
University of Strasbourg
University of Lorraine
CNRS, BETA

Preface

This book is the result of my doctoral work. My thesis, entitled "Conjuguer contrôle de gestion et créativité, une question de pratiques et de contextes organisationnels" (Combining management control and creativity, a question of practices and organizational contexts), was defended on 18 November 2019. It was prepared under the supervision of Thierry Burger-Helmchen at the BETA laboratory of the University of Strasbourg.

This research work was awarded the Honoris Causa – Special Edition "Promotion of Research in Innovation Studies" by the Innovation Research Network with ISTE Editions, "Smart Innovation". I sincerely thank the network for their interest in my work and their help in disseminating it.

This research would not have been possible without the guidance and support of Thierry Burger-Helmchen. My deepest thanks for his support, availability, and attentiveness as well as his wise and rigorous advice throughout this work.

I would also like to thank the PwC office in Strasbourg, especially Etienne Henry and Nicole Bornert, who supported me from the very beginning.

Lastly, I would like to express my gratitude to my family: Anna and Damien, Anne and Jacques, Lucile, Gauthier and Arielle, who support me every day in my activities.

July 2023

Introduction

I.1. Innovation, a way to remain competitive

In the current economic context, innovation has become a significant element in the strategies of companies and in many cases has enabled them to maintain their competitiveness, market share and growth (Porter and Ketels 2003). Thus, the development of a competitive advantage and the maintenance of performance are increasingly linked to innovation (Drucker 1985; Cohendet 1997; Bouchard and Bos 2006; Hamel and Pavillet 2012).

Innovation represents a stimulating process that pushes firms to surpass themselves and launch new products or services as quickly as possible (Chanal and Mothe 2005; Meyssonnier 2015). For Dumoulin and Simon (2005), innovation is a means of prospering by avoiding direct confrontation with dominant market players by developing a competitive advantage that represents a factor of firm survival (Schumpeter 1942; Amabile et al. 1996; Christensen 1997; Shalley et al. 2004; Anderson et al. 2014). Christensen went further by considering innovation as a factor in the survival of companies:

> Why do the smartest companies fail? Because they don't innovate enough, or badly. (Christensen 1997, p. 265)

In this context, innovation has become an integral part of business development and an essential lever for growth (Johannessen et al. 2001). It is considered a fundamental element of entrepreneurship and an element of success (Nonaka and Takeuchi 1995).

In order to achieve innovation, creativity is a necessary condition, and managing it is an essential step for organizations (Cohendet et al. 2013). Creativity and innovation are two distinct concepts with potentially different origins (Anderson et al. 2014). While creativity is about the generation of new ideas, innovation is about the implementation of creative ideas (Chang and Birckett 2004; Anderson et al. 2014).

Being creative and generating new ideas are the first steps in developing innovation. This is made possible by the creativity of employees and is necessary throughout the innovation process. The generation of new ideas, often called exploratory innovation (Benner and Tushman 2003), allows companies to develop new skills and explore new opportunities and technologies in order to satisfy new customers and existing markets. This exploratory innovation is made possible by the creativity of employees.

However, being creative and generating new ideas are not enough. Indeed, "to be creative, an idea must also be appropriate – useful and actionable", according to Amabile, in his seminal article "How to Kill Creativity" (1998). Creativity should influence the way a company runs its business, by improving a product or making a process more efficient. Finally, creativity leads to innovation if it meets the needs of consumers. For Frigo and Litman (2007), "It is not enough for the firm to be creative. The intention behind the innovation needs to be focused on the creation of new offerings that answer to needs that customers cannot get met elsewhere".

Innovation refers to the implementation of a new idea as one moves through the creative process to the operational innovation stage. During this stage, the proposals made during the creative phase are structured and channeled through multiple iterations to ensure that the new idea is transformed into value for the company and becomes a form of routine (Obstfeld 2012).

Creativity and control are antinomic by definition and sources of tension. In the management science literature, we find two opposing trends on the subject. The first trend favors the use of management control tools to manage innovation, and the second trend warns against the use of management control tools to manage innovation.

In the face of divergences and tensions in the literature, and in the absence of consensus on the type of management to adopt, it is relevant to look in more detail at the question of the management of innovation processes.

I.2. The management of innovation, a delicate balance between control and creativity

The first question to ask is as follows: do we really need to manage innovation processes? A member of the general management of a technological research center specializing in agri-food said to us: "Indicators kill creativity". The system of control and the system of creativity seem to be antinomic.

In addition to these tensions between control and creativity, other specificities also come into play and must be taken into account in the way of managing this process. For example, the nature of the innovation developed, the overall strategy of the company, the values, personality and skills of the project leaders, the expectations of the funders or even the field of activity of the organization. These parameters are an integral part of the project and condition its success. They must not be neglected during the development and evolution of the tool to ensure that it is relevant, accepted and used.

The monitoring tool would no longer be an appendix to a project, but it would become a full-fledged element of it by becoming a strategic and operational support to the innovation process.

According to Plantz et al. (1997) and Kaplan (2001), performance measures are effective tools for communicating the identity, missions and strategies of an organization. Waggoner et al. (1999), Henri (2006) and Townley et al. (2003) define performance measurement tools as examples of the shared values within an organization. These tools are used to communicate within and outside the organization. Studies have shown that these tools induce organizational change and that organizations become what they measure (Grimes 2010).

The construction of a tool and the choice of indicators then become complex, as finding a balance between the different parameters of control, creativity and project specificities, organization or stakeholders is necessary. However, they are still necessary due to the influence and support that management tools can have in the innovation process.

Such tools have yet to be invented, and it seems that applying general recipes or duplicating a relevant tool from one structure to another is not the appropriate solution. Instead, adapting the tool to each project is more judicious.

The success of an innovation depends on how people will manage its development (Cooper 1979a, 1979b; De Brentani 1991; Di Benedetto 1996; Balachandra and Friar 1997; Griffin 1997; Ernst 2002).

I.3. Objective and organization of the work

At the heart of corporate strategy, discussions on the management of creative and innovative activities naturally occur among entrepreneurs, project managers and financial managers. This particularly concerns managing efficiency within their innovation process, the different stages of the process, the balance between control and creativity, and the specific indicators and processes that could be implemented to manage innovative activities. The challenge for these actors is to not kill creativity by relying solely on standard financial criteria (Christensen et al. 2008). By considering innovation as a creative process (Barreyre 1980) from ideation to implementation of the solution, we propose to question the management of this process.

In this book, we examine the interdependencies between control and creativity and the role of the organizational context. To do so, we adopt three perspectives: descriptive, analytical and exploratory:

– The typology of managing innovation processes. In Chapter 1, we define the main concepts: innovation, the innovation process and the management of innovation processes. Then, we will review the relationships between management tools and the innovation process. In Chapter 2, we describe the tools used to manage innovation processes and meet with the actors involved in innovation and management control in organizations to gather their management practices and tools.

– The balance between formal controls and informal practices. The management of the innovation is accomplished not only through formal management control tools but also through informal practices. In Chapter 3, we study the search for balance or accepted imbalance in organizations with the analysis of three cases.

– Management control in a specific environment. The case of the social and solidarity economy (SSE). Chapter 4 proposes to broaden our study by exploring different sectors of activity where management control is also in tension. We examine the case of the SSE where management control is in tension with the need to innovate and strong human and social values.

Figure I.1 shows the organization of the structure.

Interdependencies between control and creativity: what are the roles in the organizational context?	
The typology of managing innovation processes	Chapter 1: Managing Innovation Processes, a Tension Between Control and Creativity
	Chapter 2: Management Tools of Innovation Processes
The balance between formal controls and informal practices	Chapter 3: Balance Between Formal Controls and Informal Practices
Managing control in a specific environment. The case of the social and solidarity economy	Chapter 4: Managing Control in a Specific Environment, the Case of the Social and Solidarity Economy

Figure I.1. *Organization of the book*

Managing Innovation Processes, a Tension Between Control and Creativity

In this chapter, we frame the subject. First, we define the main concepts of our research: innovation, innovation process and management of innovation processes. Then, we will review the literature with an overview of the relationships between management tools and the innovation process.

1.1. Innovation

Innovation is polymorphic and has many facets. There are many definitions and typologies in the scientific literature. The definitions of innovation vary according to the context in which they are used.

The notion of innovation was introduced by Schumpeter (1911), who defines it as the ability to develop new combinations of the firm's resources, their relationship to the market and the use that society makes of them. According to the author, it must be conceived as destructive and creative, both movements generating uncertainty. The author distinguished innovation from invention by its economic and social processes. Invention represents a solution to a problem or a technical process. It only becomes innovation when it is introduced on the market. This definition offers a broad vision of the different possible formats of innovation.

Later, Zaltman et al. (1973) define innovation as "any idea, method or material object perceived as new at its unit of adoption". In this definition, we find the notions of product and process innovations as well as the character of relative novelty.

Other authors do not see innovation as a relative novelty but as something entirely new. This is the position initially adopted by Van de Ven. This author has evolved his position, going from the representation of an innovation as a radical novelty in his early work to a relative novelty later on. According to de Ven (1986), innovation can be technical or administrative and is based on a new idea that challenges the established order or is perceived as such by the actors concerned.

Drucker (1985) also shares this view. Indeed, his definition is as follows:

> The conception and realization of something new, as yet unknown and non-existent, in such a way as to establish new economic contributions from the combination of old, already known and existing elements, giving them a new economic dimension. Innovation then constitutes the link that transforms a set of elements, each of which has a marginal efficiency, into a powerful integrated system.

Pearson (1991) provides a complementary vision by defining the two characteristics of the innovator's situation. The first is the uncertainty related to the final result, and the second is the uncertainty as to the means to be used to achieve the objective. In both cases, there is a lack of information either about the choices related to a solution that does not yet exist, or about the organization's rules of operation that allow the solution to be adopted.

Through the *Oslo Manual* (2005), the Organization for Economic Cooperation and Development (OECD) defines innovation as "the implementation by a company, for the first time, of a new or significantly improved product (good or service) or (production) process, a new marketing method or a new organizational method in the practices of a company, the organization of the workplace or relations with the outside world" (OECD 2005, p. 54).

While organizational or process innovations can certainly be levers of performance, the multifactorial nature of the levers that lead to change, the adoption curves and their effect on the organization make them more challenging to access for observation and evaluation (Dubouloz 2014).

In the context of the companies studied, we focused on product or service innovations because our interactions with these companies were limited in time. On the other hand, within the framework of the SSE organizations, we could benefit from a longer observation time, which allows us to take into account organizational innovations as well. Many authors emphasize the need to align the development of innovations with the strategy of organizations. This allows for a favorable environment for innovation (Chiva-Gomez et al. 2004) and stimulates the necessary conditions for sustained growth (Lofsten 2014).

1.1.1. *The different types of innovation*

There are different types of innovation. To present them, we take the classification again according to Le Loarne and Blanco (2009), which proposes a categorization according to the degree of disruption and the object of the innovation.

1.1.1.1. *Typology according to the degree of disruption*

Among the distinctions according to the degree of disruption, we find both incremental innovations and radical innovations (Freeman and Perez 1988).

Incremental, marginal or continuity innovations are innovations that will permanently affect the object of the innovation. These are small-scale improvements that allow companies to develop their offers by extending the life of products or services without taking many risks. There is no questioning of what exists in this type of innovation. It is the "game of small improvements to the product or process" (Durand 1992, p. 1).

Radical innovations, on the other hand, involve a major technological leap from one product to another, a rupture with the existing product, making it obsolete. It will be an upheaval in the market that requires the company to take risks and consumers to change their habits. They will change the competitive game by making it possible to "break through the barriers imposed by competitors and maintain or create competitive advantages in constantly changing markets" (Aktouf et al. 2006, p. 456).

We can also mention disruptive innovation (Christensen 1997), a more recent concept that designates an innovation that creates, transforms or destroys a market. It involves marketing products that are simpler, more practical and at a lower price than products already on the market. This type of innovation extends the consumer market and can also redefine performance standards.

The author distinguishes between the lower break and the market break. The former defines the case where the rate of improvement of new products exceeds consumers' adaptation rate to these new technologies. A similar product with lower performance but still sufficient for the consumer will be the object of this lower break. The second, market break, represents the case where the so-called "inferior" product will be suitable for a new customer segment. Christensen (1997) points out that disruptive innovations require the creation of new models. This is easier for new entrants to the market than the complexity that this can generate for an established player due to the conflict between the existing business model and the new model.

Finally, innovation efficiency is also defined by Christensen (1997). It is about putting a product similar to the existing ones on the market but at a lower price.

1.1.1.2. *Typology according to the purpose of the innovation*

Just as Schumpeter defined five types of innovation (product, process, market, organizational and raw material), the OECD, in the *Oslo Manual*, distinguishes four types of innovation:

– Product innovations that include the development of new products or new services. It is defined as "the introduction of a new good or service". This definition includes significant improvements in technical specifications, components and materials, embedded software, usability or other functional characteristics.

– Process innovations that are concerned with the use of a new production or distribution method. Le Loarne and Blanco (2009) point out that the distinction between product/service and process innovations lies above all in the question it raises: who does the firm intend to use the innovation?

– Marketing innovations that take into account changes in packaging, placement, promotion or pricing of a product.

– Organizational innovations that concern the new organizational processes that can be implemented, the organization of the workplace or the relations with the outside world.

This distinction highlights that innovation encompasses not only many actors within the company but also partners of organizations, suppliers, distributors and consumers. Each type of innovation can include different actors and is developed according to a distinct process.

Other classifications of innovations exist. We can cite the one that considers the context of the use of the innovation (Barreyre 1980). The author distinguishes innovations according to whether they are:

– of a creative process from ideation to implementation of a solution;

– a process by which a novelty will be used or adopted by a company;

– of an object considered new as a result.

This classification is interesting and complementary to the previous ones because it allows us to define the angle from which we wish to approach innovation. We choose to see innovation as a creative process going from ideation to the implementation of the solution, according to Barreyre's (1980) classification. We will develop this notion of the innovation process in the next section.

1.1.2. *Innovation, a process in several stages*

According to Adams et al. (2006), to achieve effectiveness, it is recommended that organizations establish a formal process for developing innovation. Innovation can be seen as a process, that is, a "set of activities linked together by significant flows of information (or information-carrying material [...]), and which combine to provide a significant and well-defined tangible or intangible product" (Lorino 1995, p. 112). Tidd et al. (2006) propose a definition of innovation through this process angle:

> Innovation is the process of turning an opportunity into new ideas and putting those ideas into practice, to a large extent.

Fernez-Walch and Romon (2013) also consider that "innovation is a deliberate intra- and inter-organizational process that leads to the proposal and adoption of a new product in a market or within an organization". This process allows the organization to improve its strategic position and/or strengthen its core competencies, knowledge and know-how. Midler (1993) considers the innovation process as the process of reducing uncertainty.

The notion of uncertainty, already mentioned above and linked to the fact that the innovation is likely to disrupt the market, underlines the company's risk-taking during the development of innovation. Midler emphasizes that the more the innovation process progresses, the more the weight of uncertainty will decrease.

In the literature, we find different representations of the innovation process. Barreyre (1980) speaks of a process that goes from ideation to solution implementation. Navarre (1989) refers to innovation as a project divided into four stages: emergence, conception, realization and closure. Schumpeter (1911) puts forward an innovation process model similar to the technology push model, where technology drives innovation. The market does not intervene in the innovation development, contrary to the demand-pull model, where innovation is driven by the market. In Schumpeter's model, innovation contains three main stages: basic research, invention, that is, the application of research, and then innovation in the strict sense, that is, the development of the innovation, production and marketing. Tidd et al. (2006) also propose a similar process with three stages: the search for "relevant signals", selection and implementation. The aim is to "translate the possibilities contained in the trigger idea into a new element and ensure its launch in the internal and external market". The authors point out that there may be variations by sector or type of innovation, but the underlying process remains the same.

At each stage, the purposes are different (Fernez-Walch and Romon 2013). Thus, the first stage, emergence, is characterized by creativity. The second stage, design, combines creativity and rigor and allows choices to be made about the best projects. The feasibility and expected results of the project are evaluated at this stage. Implementation is then a "rigorous management" stage that allows the construction of a solution.

However, Coombs et al. (1987) and Freeman and Soete (1997) point out that this process should not be seen as a linear system and that innovation is a process in which interaction is essential. For Tidd et al. (2006), simplifications as linear models are more like frameworks of thought than descriptive models. Kline and Rosenberg (1986) refuted the linear model and proposed a more iterative model where interaction within the firm is emphasized, as well as the back and forth that can occur during the process.

The internal and external interactions that are modeled in the representations of the innovation process reflect the new forms of this process. The latter is also adopted by practitioners, for example, at Procter & Gamble, where R&D (research and development) has become C&D (Connect & Develop). A new open innovation strategy has been put in place, enabling even more innovations to be developed. In 2006, the department's productivity increased by 60% and more than a third of new products on the market came from outside the structure.

The funnel process is a process that is spreading in companies (Le Loarne and Blanco 2009). This model, also known as the pipeline, proposes a vision that considers the iterative aspects of interactions within the company and with the outside world. Figure 1.1 represents this process.

The authors highlight two main phases, upstream and downstream. At the beginning of the project, the upstream phase is characterized by an important creativity, also called fuzzy front end (Cooper and Kleinschmidt 1987; Cooper and Kleinschmidt 1995), and the knowledge is rather tacit (Nonaka et al. 1994). In the downstream phase, we find the development of the idea and then the marketing. Ben Mahmoud-Jouini and Charue-Duboc (2014) emphasize that the marketing stage is not the end of the project. Indeed, "the sequence of commercializations of an innovation by subsidiaries located in different local contexts [...] requires adaptation each time" (Ben Mahmoud-Jouini and Charue-Duboc 2014, p. 9).

In our book, where we study the management of innovation development, we also consider innovation as a process. Tidd et al. (2006) point out that understanding innovation as a process determines how we manage it.

To represent our vision of innovation, we use the representation of the innovation according to Cohendet and Simon (2015), which we reproduce in Figure 1.2.

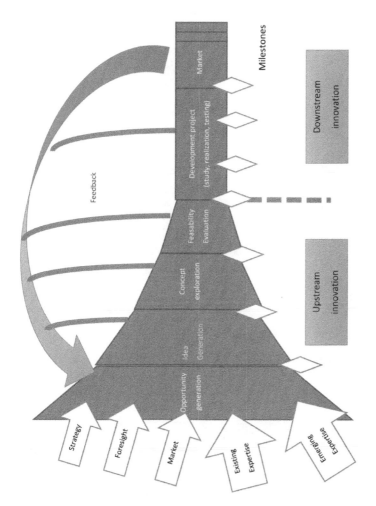

Figure 1.1. *Funnel or pipeline innovation process (source: Benoît-Cervantes 2012)*

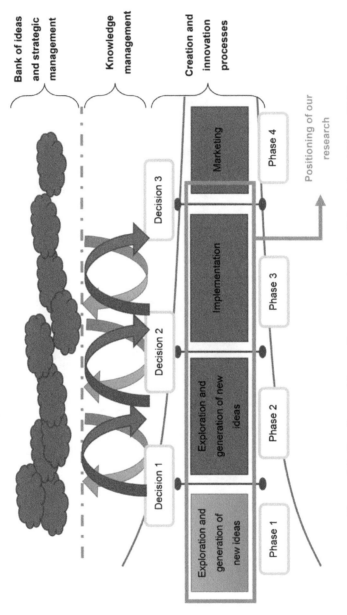

Figure 1.2. *Creation and innovation process (source: Cohendet and Simon 2015)*

The model just presented proposes several levels of creativity to innovation. Innovation is seen as a continuous process from ideation to the creation of a new product or service. The first stage of this innovation process, exploring and generating new ideas, corresponds to an exploratory phase (Benner and Tushman 2003). Exploratory innovation is defined as an innovation deployed in a logic of disruption and the creation of new knowledge or skills (Chanal and Mothe, 2005). In the representation of Cohendet and Simon (2015), this generation and exploration phase is broken down into a longer process, in parallel with the development of innovations. Knowledge management lies between these two simultaneous processes, which provides the link between the generation of ideas and the innovation process itself. After the exploration phase, the model presents the conceptualization of the idea where, once the idea is validated, a more in-depth study of its feasibility is conducted. The development and implementation of the idea constitute the third phase before the exploitation of the innovation and the market launch. This last stage also includes the phase of appropriation of the innovation by the market and its adaptation in line with the initial concept (Ben Mahmoud-Jouini and Charue-Duboc 2014).

The authors use these three levels to distinguish innovation in the territories. We reuse them here to link with the tools for managing innovation processes presented in section 1.2.

Our positioning corresponds to the lower part of Figure 1.2. The model can easily be simplified into four steps and thus be understandable for all practitioners and therefore be the source of value for managerial practice and research (Von Krogh and Grand 2000). The notions of phases and decision points are common in both the literature and the professional world.

1.2. Management tools for innovation?

1.2.1. *Management tools*

Suppose we draw a parallel between our vision of innovation and existing innovation management. In that case, we can reuse the representation of Cohendet and Simon (2015) to distinguish the different categories of management practices and tools presented in the literature. Indeed, we find a typology of different management practices for managing the innovation process. We present them in Table 1.1.

The first two categories of tools are knowledge management practices that we can relate to the two higher strata of representation of Cohendet and Simon (2015). First, they are places or venues that enable the generation of ideas.

We can define them as "ba", a "shared context", a space in which knowledge is exchanged and which will create a context favorable to the sharing and creation of knowledge. It is a dynamic process that relies on a critical relational base, and the actors must be committed to the process for this space to be productive.

Then, we find more formal knowledge management tools that will allow us to encourage the creation of new ideas.

The last category corresponds to management control practices that occur during the *stricto sensu* innovation process, that is, the bottom layer of the representation by Cohendet and Simon (2015).

We opt for a broader vision of management control that includes all formal and informal actions that influence individuals and groups to encourage them to achieve the organization's objectives.

Formal tools are control methods of an explicit nature. They are structured, written, explicit and formalized by procedures and coded by rules set up beforehand.

For Guibert and Dupuy (1997), they correspond "on the one hand to hierarchical logic based on functional and operational divisions, and on the other hand, to the standardization mechanisms associated with these divisions".

Knowledge management practices	Typologies of management practices	Objectives	Examples
	Spaces for innovation. The "ba" is a shared space, a place of interaction, which creates new knowledge (Argyris and Schön 2002)	Encourage exchanges to think outside the box and develop new ideas	Open innovation tool (Chesbrough 2006)
			Collaborative platform
			Community of practice (Wenger 1999)
			Corporate social networks
			Dedicated workspaces
			Partnership
			Working groups
			Innovation ecosystem
			...

Typologies of management practices		Objectives	Examples
Knowledge management practices (continued)	Tools	Manage innovation potential (Fernez-Walch and Romon 2013) Encourage the generation of new ideas	C-K tool (Hatchuel and Weil 1999)
			Triz tool (Altshuller et al. 1997)
			Design thinking (McKim 1980)
			Creative problem solving (Osborn 1953)
			Storytelling (Salmon 2008)
			Bisociation (Koestler 1964)
			Brainstorming (Osborn 1953)
			Scenario
			Idea sheet
			etc.

Typologies of management practices		Objectives	Examples
Management control	Formal tools	Monitor the progress of a project Arbitrate on the continuity of a project Monitor forecasted results (Berland and Persiaux 2008)	Balance scorecard (Kaplan and Norton 1992) Gantt diagram (Gantt 1913) PERT graph (Malcolm et al. 1959) Budget follow-up Reporting Milestones etc.
	Informal exchanges		Informal, unplanned exchanges around the innovation process allow decisions to be made.

Table 1.1. *Typologies of innovation process management practices*

Informal controls are implicit and trust-based mechanisms. This type of control has a social component.

Guibert and Dupuy (1997) describe this control as "the interplay of transverse, evolving, and often implicit relationships between actors or components of the organization, in the face of the emergence of new or poorly structured problems. To control is to facilitate, in an informational sense, the knowledge and sharing of the mapping of these relationships and the potentialities they present, and thus to create the conditions for self-control".

The notion of planning must also be taken into account to distinguish between formal and informal tools. The former are tools that are planned to be used. They will take the form, for example, of a monthly dashboard, a quarterly follow-up of the stage-gate, etc.

In contrast, informal practices are not planned; they can be used daily consciously or unconsciously by some actors.

Thus, a discussion around a coffee machine will allow exchanges, for example, on the progress of an innovation process and eventually lead to making decisions.

The use of these informal and formal practices can be related to the typology of control proposed by Ouchi (1979), which distinguishes between control by results, behavior and groups (or control by culture).

Constructed according to the contingency factors of control, which are the ability to measure results and knowledge of the process, this typology seems interesting to us to compare with the typologies of managing innovation processes.

Indeed, one of Ouchi's variables is knowledge of the production process. This can be compared with the innovation process, characterized by a high degree of uncertainty that decreases as the process progresses. The ability to measure the results correlates with the progress of the innovation process.

As the process progresses, the level of uncertainty decreases, and the organization can measure the predictive results of the innovation.

The control typology, inspired by Ouchi's (1979) model (Figure 1.3), proposes to distinguish between the use of formal and informal management control tools.

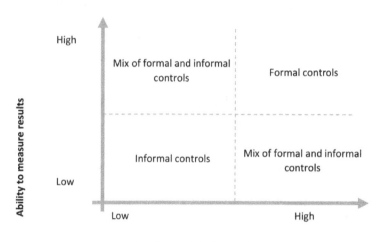

Figure 1.3. *Typology of control (source: Ouchi 1979)*

Our book focuses on these management control tools and practices that are used throughout the innovation process. We do not limit ourselves to formal tools and also study informal practices.

We place our work in line with that of Berland and Persiaux (2008). The authors conducted a 4-year study focusing on so-called high-tech innovations characterized by "the novelty of the techniques used or the complexity of their assembly" (Berland and Persiaux 2008, p. 5).

They distinguish between diagnostic and interactive controls (Simons 1995a; Simons 1995b). Diagnostic control is defined by the author as the control managed by general management, disseminating the organization's strategy via objectives that have been assigned and are measured regularly and whose deviations are monitored (Simons 1987, 1994, 1995b).

On the contrary, interactive control requires strong involvement and exchanges between the different actors. These two types of control are complementary and contribute to creating a climate of trust (Guibert and Dupuy 1997). It is necessary to find a balance between these two forms of control, as the work of Cardinal et al. (2004) has shown. Like Berland and Persiaux (2008), we are interested in managing innovations, which we consider a process.

1.2.2. *The relationship between management control and the innovation process*

The relationship between control systems and creativity is at the center of a debate among researchers in recent years.

1.2.2.1. *Management control, a support to the innovation process*

The development of innovations, currently at the heart of company strategy, has a significant impact on its performance, and we expect the need for its control to be significant. Indeed, management control is subject to different definitions that often link it to the company's strategy.

We retain that of Bouquin (1994), who defines it as "the devices and processes that guarantee coherence between strategy and concrete, daily actions". Since management control is part of corporate strategy, linking management control and innovation seems natural. Both are essential to the organization (Gilson et al. 2005; Hirst et al. 2011).

The management of innovation processes requires decisions to be made. To make them objective, management control can be used by the management team members. The monitoring tool can represent a fully fledged element by becoming a strategic and operational support to the innovation process.

Merchant (1982, p. 48) emphasizes the need to manage the development of new products:

> Controlling new product development activities is far more important in many companies than ensuring that existing products are manufactured as efficiently as possible. As a result, more resources should be devoted to controlling new product development activities, even though this area is much more difficult to control.

Janssens and Steyaert (1999) have pointed out that firms increasingly use control tools to manage instability and continuous change rather than to control stability and order.

For Drucker (2002), innovation is also a task that requires discipline. The author emphasizes that the company plays an essential role in its management by defining the objectives, proposing appropriate measurement systems and monitoring the progress of the process. It must manage innovation like any other department in the company.

For Plantz et al. (1997) and Kaplan (2001), measuring performance are also simple tools for communicating firms' strategy. Waggoner et al. (1999), Townley et al. (2003) and Henri (2006) define performance measurement tools as an example of the values shared within the organization. These are used to communicate within and outside the organization.

To this extent, the management tool, which would support the company's development-oriented strategy, could encourage the development of innovations. Simons (1995a) supports the hypothesis that tools can generate new ideas. Management control can then have a positive impact on change.

Touchais (2006) groups these actions into three categories:

– source of change;

– conveying change;

– construction and structuring of change.

Various authors have also pointed out that management tools can positively impact the development of innovations.

Abernethy and Brownell (1997) demonstrated based on case studies that in a context of uncertainty, control over people can improve performance. In the case of innovations, uncertainty is of two types (Pearson 1991):

– uncertainty about the final result: there is a lack of information about the choices to be made in relation to a solution that does not yet exist;

– uncertainty about the means to achieve this goal; there is an information deficit about the operating rules that the organization should adopt to produce this solution.

Management tools are seen as ways to manage uncertainty (Nixon 1998; Davila 2010) and coordinate new product development (Cooper 2001; Bonner 2005). Ahrens and Chapman (2004) demonstrated that control tools can support both efficiency and flexibility. Ditillo (2004), using a study of three projects in an IT company, demonstrated the role of management tools in the development of management tools. Davila et al. (2009) through a questionnaire distributed to 69 companies, also confirmed that management tools were necessary for the innovation process, particularly during the first phase of the process. Dangereux et al. (2017) are also part of this trend to reconcile management control and innovation by observing 19 innovative small and medium enterprises (SMEs).

However, management control should not be reduced solely to an instrumental approach consisting of a set of objective tools that would mainly allow for programmable decisions (Arena and Solle 2012). This seems to be all the more true when we talk about the management of innovation processes.

The challenge is to use the right types of controls and relevant indicators. For example, Davila (2000) has shown that providing information on costs and design positively impacts performance, whereas providing information on deadlines will hinder performance because formal systems limit innovation.

This being said, if finding the right control and indicator is necessary, it must also be used at the right time in the evolution of the innovation process. Touchais (2006) argues that depending on the change and the phase of its process, the place of control as a management tool is different.

1.2.2.2. *Limits of management control of innovation processes*

Other work suggests that formal management systems inhibit the intrinsic motivation to perform creative activities. In contrast, the more destructured and subtle the management mechanisms, the more efficient the creative environment will be (Anderson et al. 2014). Chiapello (1998) sees control as "an order-creating influence" in opposition to innovation because it will reduce freedom and restrict stakeholders' creativity.

According to Lenfle and Loch (2010), organizations must certainly accept a share of risk and uncertainty in managing the innovation processes. Indeed, control systems will work against creativity and harm ideation capacities (Alter 1998). This is the "perverse" effect of management tools (Berry 1983) which will influence, according to the author, a reduction of complexity, the institution of automatisms in decisions, the division of vigilance and the regulation of social relations, as well as the maintenance of coherence.

Management tools can therefore induce decisions and "behaviors beyond the control of men" (Berry 1983). Grimes (2010) confirms this vision. Indeed, his study shows that tools induce organizational changes, and organizations strive to become what they measure.

The tools can then define a framework that will be excessively rigorous and thus hinder innovation (Damanpour 1991; Touchais 2006). They represent a source of inertia that can be at the origin of organizational, behavioral and political routines, freezing the organization's functioning that some people have no interest in seeing evolve (Dent 1990). Chiapello (1997) has also pointed out in the artistic domain that creative activity is incompatible with the managerial definition of control (based on objectives and norms).

According to management's use, the tool will be able to inhibit change or, on the contrary, support it (Touchais 2006).

The tensions between control and creativity are legitimate. Fernez-Walch and Romon (2013) propose to find a balance between vision, creativity, rigor, control, order, stability and a new project characterized by instability:

> This overcoming of an apparent conflict requires the recourse to new control and measurement instruments. (Burlaud 2000)

The current literature attempts to reconcile management control and the development of innovations (Dent 1990; Berland and Persiaux 2008; Dangereux et al. 2017; Spekle et al. 2017). However, striking a balance between the two is sometimes dangerous and can lead to the following of routines, which ultimately produces very little innovation.

The company must accept the existence of imbalances at different stages of the innovation process, first between creativity and control, then, as the process progresses, between different management tools.

SUMMARY.–

Innovation is a particular project. Indeed, it is at the heart of the strategy of organizations. In this chapter, we invite the reader to consider the definitions of innovation and management control and how to combine these two antinomian notions.

We conceive of innovation as a process going from the generation of ideas to the marketing of a new product or service (Barreyre 1980). Its management is not a standard process in the organization. Its creative essence makes it a particular project (Midler 1993). Our position in the conception of innovation according to a linear process can be criticized.

Indeed, this is a simplistic vision of a much more complex project. This processual vision makes innovation appear as a project which is under control where the next step seems inevitable. The reality is different, however, as projects are subject to feedback or fail.

To overcome these criticisms, we have chosen the model of Cohendet and Simon (2015). This model allows us to take into account the existence of a creative model in parallel with the progress of innovation. The actors will thus juggle a creative environment, which is very accessible, and a more structured innovation process. This vision of innovation is more straightforward and more meaningful for innovation actors. They can find themselves in this model in the major stages of their internal processes.

As a central element of organizations, actors must drive the innovation processes to follow their progress and arbitrate on their continuity or next investments. In this work, we study its management. We focus mainly on management control practices for which we have a broad vision. Indeed, we consider them both formal tools such as balanced scorecards and budget monitoring and also informal practices. These are informal, unplanned exchanges around the innovation process in progress, allowing decisions to be made.

The combination of creativity and innovation necessary for the future of the organization, alongside the need for management and to make rational decisions, is debated in the literature.

Some authors will favor the implementation of a framework with management control practices. Others will warn of the risk of killing all creativity. Works that cross-reference the literature on innovation management and management control take into account this complexity and propose an integrating framework based on three axes: strategic management, the type of control exercised and the results of innovation control in terms of performance (Bollinger and Burger-Helmchen 2021).

This literature review does not fully answer our research question:

What interdependencies are there between control and creativity? What are the roles of the organizational context?

We organize our research into three main parts based on these theoretical foundations. The first explanatory part seeks to understand the management of innovation within organizations. The second part studies three cases of in-depth innovation processes. Finally, the third part proposes an inspiration in the social and solidarity economy where the management of innovation processes is also in tension.

2

Management Tools of Innovation Processes

In this chapter, we propose an overview of organizations' management tools and practices to manage innovation processes. Management control is the subject of many paradoxes and contradictions (Bouquin and Fiol 2007), and the management of innovation processes is one of them.

As we saw in the previous chapter, some authors go against the frameworks and controls proposed by management control tools to avoid annihilating all creativity (Chiapello 1997; Gilson et al. 2005; Touchais 2006; Christensen et al. 2008; Jørgensen and Messner 2009; Anderson et al. 2014).

However, we understand that innovation projects, which are strategic for many companies, require management oversight so that managers can see progress, make decisions and invest. The balance between control and creativity proposed by Fernez-Walch and Romon (2013) seems difficult to achieve. We question the real place of management control tools in managing innovation processes.

This work is exploratory. The first part aims to paint a picture of the role of management control tools in managing innovation processes.

2.1. The role of management tools in the management of innovation processes, a reality at two levels

To study the role of management tools in innovation management, we opted for an exploratory study in several companies. Without any preconceived ideas, we visited 11 organizations to study how they manage innovation processes.

2.1.1. *Data collection*

Data collection and analysis were carried out successively, and we conducted 16 semi-structured interviews in 11 different organizations over the period March to September 2016, which were supplemented by reading internal documents made available to us.

The sample of organizations that we were able to observe, both in terms of sectors of activity and company sizes, is very diverse. It is, therefore, a rather inhomogeneous sample, and because of this diversity, the findings should have strong validity (Royer and Zarlowski 1999).

We targeted the people who make decisions in the development process. We defined three categories of actors:

– members of management;

– members of the financial and management control department;

– members of the innovation or research and development department, closer to the operational staff.

In some organizations, we had the opportunity to meet several people in different positions, which allowed us to compare responses and consider possible differences in perception of the same management control tool. Table 2.1 presents the typology of the 16 interviews conducted in 11 organizations. These data do not constitute a statistically significant sample. However, they help paint a picture of the management control tools used in innovation development.

No.	Organization	Workforce	Sales (in millions of €)	Type of main innovation	Degree of main innovation	Position	Duration of the interview (min)
1	A: private company	10–50	Less than 1	Product	Continuity	General Management	75
2	A: private company	10–50	Less than 1	Product	Continuity	Innovation Department	80
3	B: private company	10–50	1–2	Product	Radical	General Management	60
4	B: private company	10–50	1–2	Product	Radical	Research Directorate	30
5	C: innovation laboratory	Less than 10	Less than 0.1	Product	Radical	General Management	40
6	D: technological research center	10–50	2–5	Product	Continuity	General Management	60
7	E: research center	500–1,000	2–5	Product	Radical	Research Directorate	45
8	F: private company	1,000–2,000	500–1,000	Product	Continuity	Profit Center Manager	43

No.	Organization	Workforce	Sales (in millions of €)	Type of main innovation	Degree of main innovation	Profession	Duration of the interview in minutes
9	F: private company	1,000–2,000	500–1,000	Product	Continuity	Research directorate	47
10	F: private company	1,000–2,000	500–1,000	Product	Continuity	Financial management	53
11	G: semi-public company	More than 100,000	More than 60,000	Product or service	Radical	Innovation department	40
12	H: public organization	500–1,000	100–1,000	Service	Continuity	Financial management	46
13	I: private company	1,000–2,000	2–50	Product	Continuity	Innovation department	41
14	J: private company	200–500	50–150	Service	Radical	Innovation department	100
15	K: public–private partnership	10–50	Undisclosed	Products	Radical	Operational manager	82
16	K: public–private partnership	10–50	Undisclosed	Products	Radical	Operational manager	64
Total	–	–	–	–	–	–	751 min/ 12.5 h

Table 2.1. *Description of the sample*

The questions the interviewees were asked mainly concerned the management control tools in use in their organization. Thus, for each phase of the innovation, we questioned the respondent on different control parameters:

– the presence and use of a management control tool and its format;

– the frequency of use of management control;

– the place and strategy of management control;

– the interactivity of the management control tool.

Secondary data were also collected. Several sources were used such as websites, press releases, internal documents such as organization charts, meeting minutes, and management control tools. The objective was to understand better the organization and their values as well as completing exchanges.

2.1.2. *Results obtained*

2.1.2.1. *A current topic for organizations*

All interviewees showed a research interest relevant to their current challenges. Innovation is a significant part of the organization's strategy, and they need to manage it in the best possible way. A creativity and innovation manager who we interviewed said that for them "there is no lack of ideas, we always have too many, our problem is to channel them, select them and follow their development".

For the interviewees, the difficulties in managing the innovation processes were mainly related to choosing the right indicators to obtain a management control tool for innovation. Structure H refers to indicators' selectivity and the need to avoid drowning in information. Within structure A, it is the definition of indicators that allow us to promote creativity and arbitrate on the continuity of a project that will represent a difficulty. Organization D testifies that "indicators kill creativity, the best indicators are the monitoring of turnover and the number of projects in progress. They provide a business description but do not encourage creativity, only monitor it". This question of indicators to encourage creativity was also raised with structures A, B, C and F, for whom the management control tool will not encourage creativity, while still being there to support a discussion that will encourage it. The innovation department of organization J emphasized the need for training in the face of many tools and methods for promoting innovation. Its objective is not to follow a course but to appropriate and give meaning to this aspect of the strategy.

2.1.2.2. *The existing dynamism around the subject of control management of innovation processes*

The interviews show that a real dynamic exists around management control of innovation processes and management control tools. Indeed, the recent implementation of new internal processes for innovation management, the construction of new management control tools and projects to improve existing tools or processes are common situations for most of the interviewees.

Thus, some organizations have recently implemented new management control tools or are continuously improving. For example, Organization G has implemented a new process that aims to encourage radical innovation development. A new innovation department has been created, reporting directly to the company's president, and this open innovation strategy is bearing fruit. Organization C has also recently created a structure dedicated to innovation, detached from the main organization, an innovation laboratory based on co-creation with the customer. Organization I is also working on the implementation of a new innovation management control system.

The objective is to develop innovations on the one hand, and on the other, to introduce new, more flexible, less formal working methods with fewer milestones. This new process was implemented 6 months before our interview, in parallel with the existing process, and proposes to include all employees in the idea generation phase.

Within organization A, a new management control tool of the innovation was developed in the months preceding our interview. The tool created is intended to be a discussion tool to discuss new projects.

It was set up jointly by management and operational staff. After a few months of use, the different actors had already mentioned improvement projects.

Organization H is also developing a new project. At the end of the innovation process, the monitoring tool is being built according to the project and developed according to needs. Indeed, for this organization:

> It's complicated to have a process and a methodology for managing innovation, either it's very detailed, very cumbersome and difficult to apply, or it describes intentions and we don't apply it either. The balance is complicated.

The tool that adapts as the project evolves is a common characteristic of most interviewees.

In most of the structures interviewed – A, B, C, F, G, H, I and J – the management control tools evolve as the innovation process progresses.

In the first phase of the innovation process, the idea generation phase, management practices are often informal and can be combined with more formal tools such as meeting minutes or creating idea sheets. Especially during the idea conceptualization and feasibility study phase, the second phase, more formal management control tools find their place in the different organizations. In structure G, the first phase ends with the project leader's presentation of a business plan. A presentation is requested every 3 months until the end of the process. It is evaluated according to an analysis grid that considers different themes such as the maturity of the project, the adherence to the market and the financial viability. The indicators in the analysis grid are defined explicitly according to the project and will evolve as the process goes on. Thus, financial viability is an axis of analysis that will carry more weight at the end of the project.

In organizations H and C, the management control tools are still under construction, and the indicators and management control methods are being developed as the projects progress. The interviewee from structure C described their way of managing as being "artisanal" still, the wish being to "standardize, normalize and objectify the tools". The tool has only recently been built for organization A, and the indicators are not yet fully satisfactory. These indicators are not specific to one project but are general to the entire research and development activity.

This dynamic reflects the constant search for adaptation of the companies interviewed in the face of innovation and the changes brought about by its development. In fact, these companies often face numerous elements that are difficult to measure. The question of management control of innovation processes is one that organizations still need to learn how to answer and are looking for answers to. One of the interviewees explains that "the current approaches are superficial" and that they are trying to find the best way to manage innovation. According to him, "stakeholders are not mature".

The question of the balance between control and creativity seems to be well perceived by organizations, as reflected by the Director of Research at Organization F:

> There's a balance between wanting to keep up, measuring
> without bridling or limiting the generation of ideas.

2.1.2.3. *A gap in between the beginning and the end of the interview*

At first glance, the use of management control tools seems to be completely adopted by the interviewees, but as the discussion progresses, we can see that the tools are often used because they "have to be" used.

Ultimately, decisions are not systematically made based on indicators provided by management control tools. Informal practices take on a more important role than was initially thought. Indeed, one interviewee testifies that they have "a subjective basis for evaluation" and that practices differ from project to project: "We try to harmonize the tools".

One respondent testified that despite the tools in place, decisions are made subjectively:

> We could do an evaluation that is a little less risky and a little more concrete, but we don't have the time or resources.

In addition, the process of innovation that is described linearly at the beginning of the interview – "I fully recognize our process in this four-phase process" – is no longer so at the end of the interview – "Innovation projects are very iterative projects, you have a series of trials and errors. So, you look, you test, you test a lot and you go back".

2.1.2.4. *Different expectations and needs depending on the profession*

In some organizations where we conducted complementary interviews, we had the opportunity to meet several actors in different positions.

For example, in organizations A and B, we met one person from management and one from the innovation department. These individual interviews allowed us to compare the opinions of people from different professions on the same tool. We found that Organization A had a relatively recent innovation management control system, built in the months before our interviews. Our first interview with the management person painted a relatively attractive picture of the tool in place: a tool initiated by management and the research department and management control tools defined by mutual agreement that are adapted to needs, with possible improvements, but mainly at the level of the tool's representation.

The background of the management control tool is evaluated as very pertinent by the management that uses it. The second interview, conducted with the innovation manager, gave us a very different view of the management control tool that had been implemented. The initiative to set up the tool came solely at the request of the management. During the construction of the management control tools, the opinion of the innovation manager was certainly requested but not taken into account, and no consensus was attempted to be reached. The management control tools adopted are not used by the innovation department, which is the primary addressee. The innovation manager considers the management control tool irrelevant and follows up with indicators in parallel, which are more meaningful for them and their team. This distance between management and the innovation department, as well as the difficulty of communication between these two parties, hinders productive and creative exchanges. The innovation manager confides that all proposals for new ideas must "go in the same direction" as management and that it is therefore challenging to innovate "by going outside the box". The different actors here have a different point of view and different expectations about the management control tool.

In organization B, on the other hand, the head of research and the head of the organization, although interviewed separately, are on the same wavelength regarding their opinions on the relevance of the management control tools used. This harmony can be explained by the proximity of the management to the operational staff.

In organization F, we conducted interviews with a person from the research department, a person from a profit center and a person from the finance department. Again, we find different points of view.

However, unlike organization A, the different departments accept it, and a constructive dialogue exists between them that can help improve the proposed management control tool.

2.1.3. *A two-level reality*

During the interviews, we were able to observe a discourse shift at two levels:

– between the different professions of the respondents, which reflects distinct needs and expectations;

– between the beginning and end of the interviews.

In fact, at first, the answers to the questions were relatively uniform among the respondents, despite the differences in structure, sector of activity or profile of the respondents. These responses reflected a significant use of management control tools in organizational innovation management.

Only after a certain amount of time has passed since the interview, something changes and the interviewees testify to a different reality. The management control tools are then seen as a means of communication, sometimes developed under duress. Decisions can be taken without considering the alerts provided by the indicators.

The reflection of these interviews shows a reality on two levels, a first one which is the representation of the phenomenon and a second one which is the phenomenon itself. The tools are then present to conform to the framework. Berry (1983) has highlighted this idea:

> Important changes often come from the outside, with the company's departments merely following suit: cost accounting, actualization calculations, management control, etc., were introduced under pressure from outside institutions. (Berry 1983, p. 29)

To represent this vision at two levels, we propose a representation of the management of the innovation processes using the iceberg metaphor (Figure 2.1). When we look at the management control tools and practices used, we come up against the visible part of the iceberg. This is the representation of the phenomenon, the official discourse that is communicated on the subject. The respondents describe the management control tools, procedures and techniques used. This is the image, the representation of the management of innovation processes, the official communication on the management control tools used by the organizations interviewed. These are often formal management control tools that show that the organizations rationally control the innovation process by using useful indicators. The submerged part of the iceberg represents the phenomenon actually observed in the organizations.

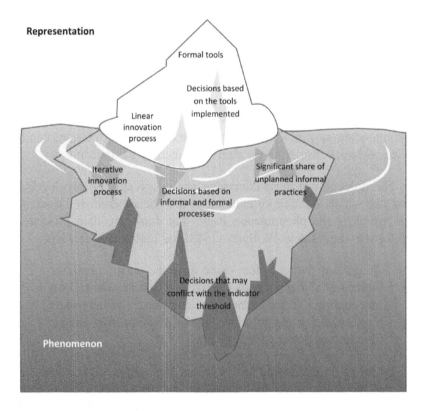

Figure 2.1. *Adaptation of the iceberg metaphor to innovation process management*

Thus, an important part of what happens is hidden. This face seems to be hidden, especially to outside eyes, by the various actors who have difficulty admitting that neither the tools put in place nor the defined processes are respected. They want to communicate about rigorous and objective management. Faced with observing a discrepancy between the representation and the phenomenon, one can legitimately wonder if the tools are fulfilling the function for which they were implemented. The interviews show that it is more complex. In fact, just because the figures don't meet the standards doesn't mean that the decision point for the next step hasn't been reached. We often find various influences (a profit center that will push the project, for example, or very aggressive competitors, which require a presence on the market) that can favor an innovation project. At the same time, the indicators of the management control tools need to be more conducive to innovation.

2.2. A quantitative analysis of the use of formal tools and informal practices

In the previous section, we could put forward a representation of managing innovation processes like an iceberg. The tip of the iceberg represents a type of management widely used by organizations with a linear innovation process, using formal tools and decisions based on these tools. The submerged part represents a different reality with an iterative innovation process, using informal practices and decisions that are not necessarily in line with the indicators. Following this finding, we extended our study of the representation of this phenomenon. We thus conducted an exploratory study on management control systems to manage innovation processes. The main objective was to define the tools and practices used during the process according to the typology of the organizations and innovations.

2.2.1. *Data collected*

We were interested in a large population of companies based on the DFCG directory, which groups together French companies with everyday issues. We targeted all organizations developing new products or new services.

Through electronic dissemination – 1,971 questionnaires were sent out – we obtained 169 responses from May to October 2016. Targeted individuals who did not respond to the questionnaire were followed up by email. The typology of respondents to the questionnaire is presented in Table 2.2.

Business sector	Company size	Type of innovations	Position
27% Manufacturing industry 14% Scientific research and development 13% Specialized scientific and technical activities 11% Trade activities The remaining sectors are represented by less than 10% of companies per sector	11% Large enterprises 68% Small and medium enterprises 21% Micro enterprises	71% Incremental innovations 25% Radical innovations 71% Co-innovation	32% Research management and operational staff directly related to research 34% Financial management 26% General management 4% Consultants 4% Other

Table 2.2. *Typology of respondents to the questionnaire*

Table 2.3 summarizes the different types of questions proposed in the questionnaire. The objectives of these questions and the possible relationships between them are summarized.

Objectives and possible relationships	Questions
To classify organizations according to sector of activity, number of employees, turnover, type or degree of innovation. Determine if certain types of organizations have needs in terms of innovation process management or if, on the contrary, certain types of organizations already have efficient tools.	Analytical questions.
To determine if the tools are evolving with the characteristics of the project or if this could be an asset.	For each phase of the process, we ask the respondent whether the tool is standard or scalable according to the characteristics of the project.
To determine the control variables that can be used in the construction of the tool and that are mainly used.	For each phase of the process, we ask the respondent about different control parameters (format of the control – formal or informal – frequency of the control, control strategy, interactivity of the tool).
To determine if the tools are at the service of the innovation process by promoting creativity or the success of innovations.	We ask the respondent's opinion on this point about the tools in place.
To determine if the tools are relevant or if improvements can be made.	We question the respondent on the relevance of the tools put in place, on the areas of improvement of the monitoring in place, and on the difficulties encountered concerning the management of the innovations.

Table 2.3. *Different types of questions proposed in the questionnaire*

2.2.2. *Results obtained*

We performed a cluster analysis to re-group the companies according to their tool use behavior. The objectives were as follows:

– to establish groups of companies according to some of their characteristics illustrated by their answers to our survey;

– to test the hypothesis of the equality of the variables relating to the use of management control tools of the innovation processes between the different groups obtained following the partitioning of the firms in the sample.

2.2.2.1. *A desire to distinguish between practices according to organization and innovation*

This analysis of discriminating variables shows that behavior is similar in the use of management control tools among the distinct groups of companies. These results show that the use of formal, informal or mixed types of tools is very similar between the established groups in terms of product and service innovation, except for informal tools which are used differently when the firm develops service innovations both upstream and downstream of the process.

2.2.2.2. *Different tools depending on the progress of the innovation process but similar according to the organizations*

Since the results obtained from the questionnaire are similar between firms of different types of firms (partitioning analysis), we conducted additional analyses on the general use of management control tools of the innovation process for all the firms in the sample.

2.2.2.2.1. The use of management control tools

Eighty-six percent of the respondents to the questionnaire felt that management control tools could promote successful innovation, and 54% of the respondents felt that the tools could promote creativity. These figures show that tools can have a real impact in supporting the development of innovations.

For small structures, we note that they put more tools in place between the first and second phases of the innovation process, which are formal.

However, unlike the larger structures, these formal tools are not implemented to the detriment of the informal tools that may exist. Between phases 3 and 4, we see a significant decrease in the use of informal practices. Phase 4 corresponds to the market launch phase, with less uncertainty and a tendency to use more traditional tools.

In large structures, we see that organizations are putting in place more, mainly formal, tools to the detriment of informal practices. This is a phenomenon that we do not find in small organizations.

For respondents who do not use tools, the desire to implement a management control tool in phases 3 and 4 of the innovation process is strong (>60%).

If this desire is felt, studying the obstacles to this implementation is interesting.

The main obstacles identified are the following:

– lack of time and financial resources (65%);

– non-compliance of the practice with the corporate culture (12%);

– the non-adherence of all the actors involved in managing the innovation process to the implementation of the tool (8%).

2.2.2.2.2. The format of the tool and the indicators used

Throughout the process, formal tools are most often used (66%). Informal tools are not neglected, as they are used by 39% of the respondents. The combined use of formal and informal tools is well established, representing 20% of control formats.

For phases 2 and 3, conceptualization and implementation, we find a majority of formal tools (24%) but again with a presence of informal tools (20%).

By phase 2, the combination of the two formats is no longer used significantly. At the time of marketing, formal tools are used in most cases.

Table 2.4 lists the management control tools and informal practices that are most used in organizations according to the stage of the innovation process. The formal/informal classification comes from the responses and is not a categorization a priori.

	Exploration and idea generation	Conceptualization of the research	Implementation	Market launch
Formal tools	Time tracking Expense tracking Tracking of idea value metrics through integrated Excel-type tools Hearing and rating of project leaders	Drafting of specifications Monitoring of costs Monitoring of deadlines Calculation of an ROI Testing of prototypes with customers and analysis of customer feedback	Cost tracking Tracking of human hours Follow-up of the deadlines ROI tracking Customer feedback Follow-up of the realization of a schedule of conditions	Follow-up of the turnover Margin tracking ROI tracking Tracking the number of customers Analysis of customer and employee feedback. Analysis of the relevance to the target of the quality of the service provided and the cost/service ratio
Informal practices	Sharing work in progress within a virtual community Innovation challenge organization	Team update, discussions	Team update, discussions	Team meetings Discussion with users

Table 2.4. *Management control tools and informal practices*

2.2.3. *A balance to be found between management control and creativity*

The analysis of the questionnaire results shows a majority use of formal management control tools. Information practices are implemented in a complementary way, mainly at the beginning of the innovation process.

The results do not raise any doubts about using formal management control tools, so we place ourselves in the first part of the literature, alongside the authors, in favor of using management control tools. The respondents did not mention in their answers the idea that the tools could harm creativity. Instead, similar to the work of Adler and Chen (2011), Dangereux et al. (2017) and Spekle et al. (2017), they are seen as a real support to innovation. However, as shown by the work of Dangereux et al., the networking of innovation processes is not only an instrument; it is also a mix of tools and practices. Indeed, informal practices are included, as we find informal, unplanned exchanges regarding the innovation process in the results of the questionnaire, allowing decisions to be made. Informal practices are used in conjunction with management control tools by the organizations. The notion of a management control system, of a "package" (Malmi and Brown 2008), seems to be particularly well suited to the definitions provided by the respondents to the questionnaire because we find in companies a conglomerate of tools and practices that coexist to meet the challenges of monitoring innovation processes.

By taking a broader view of all tools and practices, as a control system or package (Malmi and Brown 2008; Broadbent and Laughlin 2009; Ferreira and Otley 2009) with formal control tools but also informal modes of control (Guibert and Dupuy 1997; Chenhal 2003; Malmi and Brown 2008), the management control tool is not reduced to its calculation aspect and capacity for economic evaluation; it is integrated into a more global, open and dynamic control system. Management control systems are composed of a set of accounting and non-accounting processes, rules and values, formal tools and informal practices to verify the good link between strategic planning and operational management. The notion of "package", as defined by Malmi and Brown (2008), brings together the different systems that may have been put in place at different times and by different groups of actors whose interests may sometimes diverge.

The whole created could be more coherent and unified. The control system in place is an assembly of tools, techniques and practices, a device whose objectives are to control the behaviors and decisions of other actors in the organization, to ensure that they are consistent with its objectives and strategy. Each system operates in a semi-autonomous way and is articulated in different ways in different organizations. The effectiveness of control packages appears to be context dependent (Bedford et al. 2016).

The analytical framework defined by Malmi and Brown (2008) proposes five dimensions in which control systems can be placed: administrative control, strategic control (planning), cybernetic control, control through culture and managerial control (with a system of rewards and remuneration). This prism for reading management control systems proposed by Malmi and Brown (2008) has the advantage of considering multiple points of view and limiting blind spots. In the context of innovation, the points of view are multiplied because of the plurality of professions of the actors working on the project. We then study the organizational phenomenon in a more extensive system.

Box 2.1. *Control packages (source: Malmi and Brown 2008)*

The balance between management control tools and informal practices depends on the progress in the innovation process. Indeed, the formal tools are more important as the process progresses. The more the innovation process advances, the less uncertainty there is and the more management control tools find their place. We find informal practices which complement management control tools and which are more important at the beginning of the process, when the project is uncertain. The questions that organizations need to ask themselves then relate to the balance to be struck between informal practices and management control tools: how to make them coexist between informal practices and management control tools? How to make them coexist to move the innovation process forward, reduce the risk of the innovation process and reduce uncertainty while guaranteeing creativity? The reconciliation begun by Berland and Persiaux (2008), Dangereux, Chapellier and Villesèque-Dubus (2017) and Spekle, Van Elten and Widener (2017) is relevant today in companies looking for the best balance between control and creativity, forecasting and uncertainty, framework and freedom. This vision of balance is a positive one and helps to overcome the existing divide and tensions between control and innovation.

SUMMARY.–

The management control literature brings out a group of authors who favor management control tools to drive innovation and a second group warning of the dangers of mixing creativity and management control. This chapter provides an overview of the management control tools and informal practices in organizations for managing innovation processes.

First, we have brought a vision of the management of innovation processes with the iceberg metaphor (Bollinger 2020). This illustrates a reality at two levels where the existing formal management control tools, used and accepted, are the tip of the iceberg. The more informal, widely used practices represent the submerged part.

Then, in order to have a broader vision, we conducted a quantitative study with 169 people, from general management, research or financial departments to project managers or other operational staff in the research field. They come from a wide variety of organizations in terms of staffing levels, sales figures generated and sector of activity and are developing product or service innovations, these being continuous or radical. Our ambition was to be able to detect differences in practices between organizations based on statistical and economic analyses. We conducted a partitioning analysis of the sample of companies studied according to some of their characteristics (size and sector of activity) and some of their behaviors (product, service or co-innovation). While there is no doubt that management control tools have their place in the management of innovation processes, the analysis of the questionnaire and the typology of innovation process management show a convergence of behaviors and practices (Bollinger and

Martinez-Diaz 2022). Formal management control tools are widely used in organizations, complementing informal practices. We have not identified any significant differences between them according to their characteristics or the typology of innovations. Concerning the two trends identified in the literature, the respondents to the questionnaire fall into the first trend, favoring management control tools. They are seen as a structure and an aid to the innovation development process.

However, the data analysis does not reveal any significant difference according to the type of structure questioned, the respondent's profession or the degree of disruption of the innovation developed. These convergent practices raise questions. Will the development of a breakthrough innovation allow using the same type of management control tools as the development of an incremental innovation? Do small and large organizations that do not have the same resources to devote to project management have the same control structure? We can wonder about the existence of a phenomenon of mimicry. This would imply that small organizations, in a desire to display model management, would tend to respond positively to using management control tools. This response could give them a certain legitimacy (Meyer and Rowan 1977; DiMaggio and Powell 1983).

In addition, this chapter is insufficient to provide recommendations for using management control tools or informal practices to an organization. We need to find out how often and how intensively they are used or practiced. To what extent do they help in making decisions?

We then set the stage for the next chapter, which proposes a qualitative approach and will enable us to determine the individual and organizational motivations for choosing tools and practices this work identifies. Although management control is used in organizations to manage innovation processes, the fact remains that innovation and control are in confrontation, and we believe that a better balance between the two must be sought, notably through mutual understanding and convergence of points of view (Raedersdorf and Bollinger 2019).

3

Balance Between Formal Controls and Informal Practices

In Chapter 2, we highlighted the representation of managing innovation processes like an iceberg. In this metaphor, the emerged part corresponds to a representation of the management of innovation processes. This is the official discourse where management control tools are widely used and where the management of innovation processes rationally takes place by using useful indicators.

The submerged part of the iceberg represents the phenomenon observed in organizations. In this second part, the situation is more complex: the innovation process is iterative and decisions are based on informal practices sometimes contradicting the indicators of the management control tools. This representation leads us to question two aspects:

– In a phenomenon of mimicry, do organizations communicate a homogeneous representation of the innovation processes, a similar behavior, with an important use of formal management control tools?

– When making decisions in the innovation process, do organizations rely more heavily on information practices than formal management control tools?

We will answer both of these questions in this chapter and draw on the study of three organizations: Bricolo, Telco and Fluido[1]. In each of these organizations, we study the management of strategic innovations for these organizations.

3.1. A qualitative analysis of the management of innovation processes

3.1.1. *Data collected*

The three cases we study are presented in Table 3.1. All the organizations have recently developed disruptive innovations, strategic for their future.

Bricolo developed the three-wheeled lawnmower. Telco worked on the LoRa network. Finally, the last structure, Fluido, which is smaller in size, has developed a new flow measurement device that does not require any sensor in the measuring tube.

We conducted semi-structured interviews as the main means of data collection. They allow us to understand the organizational reality as perceived by the actors (Giordano 2003).

These interviews were mainly conducted with management controllers, innovation directors, general managers and project managers.

During these exchanges, we also collected all the documents relevant to the understanding of the management of the studied innovation projects (dashboard, minutes of meetings, planning, presentation of the projects, etc.).

Table 3.2 shows the different interviews conducted, as well as the observation and visit times.

---

1 These names are pseudonyms.

Organization	Sectors of activity	Market positioning	Sales in €M	Workforce	Type of innovation	Innovation studied
Bricolo	Do-it-yourself and decoration	Third worldwide group in the sale of consumer goods for DIY and decoration	10,000–30,000	More than 100,000	Disruptive innovation	Three-wheeled mower
Telco	Telecommunications	World leader	30,000–50,000	More than 100,000	Disruptive innovation	New Internet of Things network
Fluido	Manufacture of technical and scientific instruments	World leader in fluid measurement, control and regulation technology	2–50	Between 100 and 500	Disruptive innovation	Flow measurement device requiring no sensor in the measuring tube

Table 3.1. *Presentation of the three cases studied*

Organization	Interview code	Role	Interviews (min)	Visits (min)	Observations (days)
Bricolo	A1	IT Architect	–	60	–
	A2	Project Manager 1	67	–	–
	A3	Innovation Project Manager Intrapreneurship	87	–	–
	A4	Project Manager 2	63	–	–
	A5	Management Controller	95	–	–
	A6	Bricolab Project Manager	30	–	–
	A7	Observation	–	–	3
Fluido	B1	Innovation Manager	60	–	–
	B2	R&D Manager	90	–	–
	B3	Innovation Manager	–	60	–
	B4	Project Manager	70	–	–
	B5	Management Controller	93	–	–
	B6	Innovation Director	132	–	–
	B7	Marketing Manager	85	–	–
	B8	General Manager	94	–	–
	B9	Innovation Manager	120	–	–

Organization	Interview code	Role	Interviews (min)	Visits (min)	Observations (days)
Telco	C1	Innovation Director	55	–	–
	C2	Innovation Director	–	120	–
	C3	Innovation Department	–	–	1
	C4	Innovation Director	90	–	–
	C5	Project Manager	120	–	–
	C6	Transformation Manager	64	–	–
	C7	Innovative Project Manager	70	–	–
Total	–	–	1,485	240	4
			24.75 h	4 h	4 days

Table 3.2. *Summary of data collected*

3.1.2. *Results obtained*

3.1.2.1. *The use of management tools*

In the three organizations studied, we observed the use of formal tools by all actors. Fluido, Telco and Bricolo have all set up a project monitoring meeting in which the various decision-making bodies must present innovations and keep formal and compulsory indicators.

The controller at Fluido (B5) testifies to the use of two formal tools that have recently been put in place:

– a specific project management software, Sciforma, which is used to monitor costs, investments and hours spent;

– a return on investment (ROI) calculation in an Excel spreadsheet.

For her, implementing these tools is a real opportunity for the organization. Quite recently, the implementation of tools went hand in hand with obtaining a research tax credit and aid from the public investment bank. She explains:

> We were not yet very well equipped, so it was considered a constraint. We had to tinker a bit and it was quite cumbersome. But in the end, the project managers found that it was a good thing because they were forced to break down the process, to ask themselves questions.

These tools have shown that the company "does not stop projects enough and that teams sometimes tend to be too optimistic about the technical outcome and do not say stop, we spent €500,000 or €1,000,000 in investment, the project is not progressing, we must go in another direction".

For the innovation director (B6), Sciforma was set up to have a centralized tool, an overview of all the company's projects. Working in project mode, their number has increased and the idea was to have an overall view of the projects, and their progress, to be able to prioritize and manage each project.

The management controller at Bricolo (A5) also testifies to the recent introduction of formal tools: "It's new, we want to formalize, to be standard". For him, the idea is to have "a small framework, we don't limit them on customer uses, the ideas they have". The figures that must necessarily be followed are as follows: development costs, purchase gain and return on investment.

He explains that the project manager has to fill in everything because the management controller does not, unlike Fluido. In Bricolo, the management controllers challenge and assist the project managers, but they do not replace them. The project manager of Bricolo (A2) testifies:

> There was also a formal indicator that we followed closely. It was the number of product managers we had with us, that is, the number of order expectations we could have. Every month, we made a new estimate. From the moment we went looking for everyone, we always had more resources. The management always supported us because it wasn't just an innovative product, it was guaranteed sales. It was the main indicator and a negotiating force with industry. So we were always faced with the indicator of sales in terms of volume.

The project manager explains that the return rate and satisfaction indicators were strong. The different actors at Bricolo agreed that their brief at the beginning of the project allowed them to formalize the expectations and, for the first time, to set a very good framework for developing the innovation. The management controller (A5) says, "A successful brief is a successful project and an imprecise brief is precise bullshit". The project manager agrees with this idea as he explains:

> Usually when we get a brief, it's not built. This was the first time we were able to prioritize the projects.

At Telco, the formal tools in place are also used and accepted by the actors. The project manager (C5) testifies that, like at Bricolo, "a business unit must sponsor the project", which guarantees future customers. In addition, they are not allowed to leave a project without an update for more than 6 months: they have to explain and be accountable. In all three companies, much emphasis is placed on project follow-up meetings. These are formal, planned meetings with an agenda that allow decisions to be made. At Telco, these meetings are called boards, the project manager (C5) explains:

> A board is set for a given date; when you need or have to present a subject to the board, you must sign up. Boards are meetings that last 3 to 4 hours and the teams come in one after the other. We are asked not to exceed 15 to 20 minutes. Ten minutes of presentation, 10 minutes of questions and answers and then it's the next team's turn.

To stay within the time limit, Telco trained all of its project managers in the art of the pitch. The project manager interviewed testified that following his first pitch to the board, a person attending the meeting by phone said:

> It's completely crazy, there are two guys who arrived, they talked for five minutes, they presented a lamp and they left with €400,000, I've never seen that.

According to the project manager, their training and how they presented the project were key success factors. In terms of indicators, at Telco, the creation is done in a collegial way. The project manager testifies:

> If indicators, in the way they are designed and with what they say, are not shared, they are questioned. There is necessarily a consensus phase.

The various people interviewed know that tools are necessary to manage innovation processes. The head of innovation at Fluido testifies:

> The project manager is a leader in using the tools in place. They are aware of their price and importance and the value of working together.

However, depending on the business, the use of the tools is more or less constrained. Fluido's management controller (B5) explains that when the project managers want to, especially before certain decisions are made, they can come and see her and make cost calculation scenarios according to the different options.

She explains that some project managers "go through these moments; others have really integrated it and come upstream as soon as they think that what they're planning to change will impact the cost". For her:

> Naturally, the cost of the project is not a problem for some of the project managers. The important thing for them is to get things done, to get a technically operational product. And the fact that they meet a market or respect the costs is far from them, even if it is increasingly important.

The marketing manager of Fluido (B7) testifies that the tool "allows for better management; it has the merit of framing them even if it is not a miracle solution because the projects do not progress faster". For the second project manager at Bricolo (A4), the tools "are mainly used to inform and reassure, but do not help her in her daily work". The innovation manager at Fluido (B6) is careful not to put too many tools in place because "indicators and processes are barriers".

3.1.2.2. Evolving tools

The tools have been put in place recently in the three cases studied and will continue to evolve.

At Bricolo, the innovation project manager testifies that "the tools built themselves as the project progressed". The management controller had the same testimony.

The same phenomenon is observed at Telco and Fluido. In the latter case, ad hoc indicators are built as they go along. The project manager (A4) explains, "As far as the definition of indicators is concerned, we create them as we go along according to needs. We try to find an answer and we put the indicator in place". In each case, a slide is mandatory during project presentations, and then the project managers are free to add the necessary indicators. The Telco project manager (C5) explains that each time there was a malfunction, a new indicator was created and when the problem was solved, they removed the indicator. It was by walking about that the indicators were found. At Bricolo, we find the same vision of indicators. The innovation manager said that with this project, they "had to wipe the slate clean; everything was built up as we went along, and we have things to improve". Bricolo's management controller has a more definite opinion on the matter. For him:

> There is a basic rule in the process. It is that the process must not adapt; it is up to the teams to adapt to the process because it is structuring. The process does not constrain; it liberates people. This is what we need to understand and this is what I am trying to explain here.

However, the tools in place are not necessarily the most suitable, and the various players know this. In Fluido, the marketing manager (B7) does not really use Sciforma, he explains:

> Yes, I use it occasionally when I need to carry over the hours I've spent on a project. But it doesn't get used more than that.

He explains that the timelines outlined and discussed in meetings are rarely met. They lose credibility if they communicate it to customers or vendors, but the product is slow to come out. The general manager (B8) does not really use it either, calling it "very average". The project manager is not satisfied either; he uses an Excel file to track his project in parallel. He (B4) explains:

> I fill it out, I'm forced to, but oh well. It's also good to do a monthly report, so every month I put in the costs, the hours spent on the projects, the investments and the progress of the project.

The controller regrets the lack of interactivity in Sciforma with the indicators. The innovation manager is aware of these biases. In his eyes, the tool was planned to monitor all the projects but is heavy and not user-friendly. He agrees that it is not pleasant for the project manager who must use it every day. He also raises a second problem: it is a very specific tool to Fluido, and it has undergone a lot of development to meet the company's expectations. But, if the teams call the hotline, they cannot answer because they have too many specifications. The same applies to new versions for which it is necessary to pay for customization.

The calculation of the ROI is not optimal either. The controller (B5) explains:

> We moved to a calculation that came too early and was too rigorous. It's normal for the project manager to have a hard time adhering because we are too early. We tried to do something but it doesn't reflect reality; we're doing it to fill the box.

She is surprised that the group constrains the indicators, but that they are not followed when it comes to making decisions. She explains:

> I am convinced that this project is the future of our site; however, if I am doing hard financial calculations, I am not. At no time at Fluido has a project been stopped because the financial indicators were bad.

The meetings organized at Fluido are not satisfactory either. The general manager notes that few decisions are discussed, even though it is basically a decision-making body. He regrets that very technical topics are discussed.

Thus, the various organizations are considering areas for improvement. For the marketing manager at Fluido (B7), it is necessary to formalize the informal and "avoid that decisions taken around the water cooler are not communicated to everyone, because then people say they don't know or pretend not to know". The general manager (B8) of the structure tries to transmit basic reflexes:

> Thinking about customers, thinking about values, that we systematically weigh a cost against a value, that we think before doing it, not to set deadlines that are too restrictive, and that if it is necessary to do an additional study which adds another month, we do it.

The controller (B5) would like to track inventory, she explains:

> Inventory tracking is an indicator that is not tracked in Sciforma or the ROI calculation. To launch a new product, we have to overstock; we are obliged to stock. This is becoming a problem because the stock level for research and development is high. It also poses a problem for depreciation issues because the parts are not rotating.

The Director of Innovation (B1) seeks "soft" indicators. He defines them as "indicators where people can relate, see their use and impact, realize the issues, and know the project's history".

3.1.2.3. *Informal practices to compensate for the need for formalism*

In each case studied, the interviewees highlighted the management carried out by informal practices. At Telco, it is the project itself that originated in informal exchanges. The project manager (C5) said:

> The birth of the project, between R. and I, was done at the water cooler and became Telco's strategic development. It's exciting when it happens like that. It can't be all strategic, all known, all planned. We were one desk apart and we started thinking that I knew how the network worked and he was wondering if people couldn't deploy it themselves. So the idea was to have a technology that allows a collaborative network deployment mode, where the customers deploy part of the network. It was already something innovative and then we asked ourselves what service we could put on it. I think the space as it was designed really helps with the idea creation. In a place like the 3rd one, the lab, I met

the person who helped us develop this tool. If it wasn't for this place, I wouldn't have met him and the development wouldn't have been the same. It's a place for cross-fertilization.

But informal practices take place throughout the project at Telco. Before each formal presentation, the project manager explains to us that he will informally present the project and its challenges to the people making the decisions. This allows for discussion, and to raise problematic points upstream. The only area where informal discussion was unnecessary was security, when the lamp was integrated into the network. The interviewee explains:

When we had to pass the security audit, there was no room for error. The network at Telco can't be informal, it's the heart of our company, it's its DNA. We had a combination of informal and formal depending on the subject.

The most informal part was used at Telco for this project:

When we were solving the problems of lost messages, we developed tools to analyze the problems ourselves. Since the technology was new, we did everything ourselves and were at a total standstill. We went to someone who wasn't very busy and whose skills we were interested in. The person was very motivated, and we created a tool that didn't exist, and it was all informal.

Informality is also found at Fluido, where the marketing manager explains that for him, what makes projects move forward are the little water cooler meetings or lunches between colleagues. The project manager is aware of the importance of informal discussions, of feeling. He testifies that at Fluido:

Costs are not what will make a decision. Of course when it comes to an investment, we're going to think in terms of the budgets used, but those are not the key indicators.

Finance appears to be a support function and does not participate in all the follow-ups; the interventions are ad hoc. The project manager also practices informal exchanges, especially at the beginning of the project; these are standing meetings, about 10 minutes long, where each person presents their progress from the previous day. The objective is to inform, exchange, but not expose problems that are too technical. The management controller (B5) confirms that the informal approach works very well when it takes place internally. Still, it complicates relations when people from distant sites are involved in the project. The innovation manager (B6) explains that informality plays a significant role in the innovation department, and has strongly encouraged the development of informal practices as compensation for the framing demands imposed by management. He cites as an example:

> We were asked to put Sciforma on; our response was to create technology circles to share with the communities informally. This was done in parallel. I want the informal part to remain important; we are now in open space following a reorganization.

Informal practices are also present at Bricolo. When we asked the project manager what tools were available to him to manage the projects, he (A4) answered as follows:

> The most important tool is trust. The success of this project depends on trust everywhere, at all levels. Without trust, we would have had nothing within the design team, with management, between the business units and then with the industry. Then, we had to have a lot of rhythm, we had regular and unexpected meetings with the product managers, often outside, on the lawns in front of a prototype. The impact of these off-the-cuff meetings was tremendous. If anyone had any doubts, all they had to do was test it. The process was greatly accelerated because of this.

For the innovation project manager, one of the primary indicators, not measurable as such, is the motivation and the temperament of the people behind the project, and it is not so much the idea that counts as the people. The controller also recognizes that there is a great deal of informality in the decision-making process. He explains that there are *go* or *no-go* criteria, but everything is discussed in the end.

3.1.2.4. *The consensus to confirm intuition*

In all three organizations, we see that management tools exist, that they are not entirely satisfactory and that decisions can be made based on exchanges and informal practices. The marketing manager at Fluido (B7) explains that his decision-making is often "the stomach talking". The project manager also testifies that he relies heavily on his feeling. The intuition present at Fluido we also find at Bricolo and, to a lesser extent, at Telco, which is certainly more mature in managing innovations.

This way of making decisions based on one's own feelings is accompanied by a search for consensus. The general manager at Fluido testifies that this desire to reach consensus is in the company's genes. One of the objectives of the innovation director is to reduce the time spent in meetings, a time that is now too important because of this desire to reach consensus. At Bricolo, the search for consensus traditionally slows down the process. However, according to the project manager, holding external meetings with a prototype helped to find a consensus more quickly, to convince. He (A4) testifies that this was the first time he managed to "get Poland, Russia, France, Spain and Italy together on a joint project. Everyone was around the same table".

This search for consensus confirms the intuitions of the different actors but also has its drawbacks, such as the fact that some people may give up on their opinion because they have less power. In contrast, others may have feelings of frustration, this finally favoring political games and lobbying. The project manager (B4) at Fluido testifies:

> Yes, absolutely, I do some lobbying but not too much. I contact the various members informally in anticipation of decisions being made. We discuss on the phone, by

e-mail or between two meetings the difficulties and solutions that I foresee and we discuss them together to trim down already. People are rarely surprised, when they arrive at the meeting; they have already seen things.

The project manager at Telco (C5) also testifies that during a preboard, we try to find a consensus:

The smartest project managers will lobby on the side to give their project a better chance.

The Telco project we studied was a strategic project for the firm. The project manager testifies that they took advantage of this situation:

Sometimes we played with it, when someone would say no, you're not going to have access to that data, we would just say, "You do what you want; SR [Telco CEO] supports the project, and if you need us to bring this up to a level where it's going to get a little complicated, you can try". So that was a lot of negotiating power; without abusing it, you have to use it too because innovating sometimes is disruptive.

3.2. Management under construction

3.2.1. *Managing with full awareness*

To answer the first question, which questions the fact that the organizations communicate a homogeneous representation of innovation processes, a similar behavior, with an important use of formal management control tools, we have put forward the neo-institutional theory (DiMaggio and Powell 1983). This theory assumes that in an uncertain environment, all organizations will tend to adopt similar behavior according to a mimetic isomorphism.

The case studies show us that all the players use management control tools, each of them imposing indicators that must be presented during progress meetings, with a whole slide that is mandatory, standardized and includes calculations of indicators such as ROI, for example.

However, we also show that organizations are not fooled. They will certainly communicate at first glance about tools and practices that seem similar, but when we study them through case studies, it turns out that the systems have specificities linked to the context of the innovation, specific to each organization.

Innovation being the spearhead of many organizations, managing innovation processes is strategic. The work of Mintzberg et al. (2005) highlights the importance of the role of the leader in the deployment of the organization's strategy. His role is decisive in the way he directs and conducts critical activities.

Innovation is an integral part of the strategies claimed by organizations, and its management is not exempt from the strategist's vision. According to research in anthropology, a phenomenon of mimicry is inherent to all human behaviors and therefore to any strategic decision (Girard 1972).

Mimicry refers to an adaptive reflex behavior, unlike imitation, a voluntary and intentional action (Baudonnière 1998). This approach seems interesting in the case of innovation, which represents an unstable and uncertain context. This concept has indeed been used in different theories to respond to uncertainty. This is the case of the neo-institutional theory (DiMaggio and Powell 1983), of the theory of cascading information (Banerjee 1992; Bikhchandani et al. 1992) or of the theory of conventions (Gomez 1996).

Thus, in uncertain contexts with little visibility on the consequences of one's choices, as innovation can be, authors agree on the observation of a convergence of behaviors (DiMaggio and Powell 1983; Galaskiewicz and Wasserman 1989; Haverman 1993; Gomez 1996; Lieberman and Asaba 2006).

Lieberman and Asaba (2006) argue that this phenomenon must be of rational interest, that is, economic and calculative. Depending on the approach, it would be conditioned by different interests.

Thus, in the theory of cascading information, it is a question of research for maximizing gains in a risk situation, rationality being guided toward a calculation and an instrumentalization. In convention theory, rationality is more evaluative. Gomez (1996, p. 67) emphasizes that "imitating what one believes to be the normative behavior is the reasonable solution to uncertainty".

According to the neo-institutional approach, this homogenization of behaviors is the result of an institutional isomorphism which is explained by three movements according to the model of DiMaggio and Powell (1983):

– Mimetic isomorphism, where organizations will imitate the practices of other similar or model companies. Mimicry would be sought after as a result of symbolic and ritual motivations rather than rational ones (Lieberman and Asaba 2006), in particular by guaranteeing the legitimacy of the organization's activities (Meyer and Rowan 1977; DiMaggio and Powell 1983) or by reducing uncertainty regarding the actions to be taken (Moquet 2005). Legitimacy is defined here according to Suchman's (1995) definition wherein legitimacy is a generalized perception that an organization's actions are appropriate, desirable and consistent with a system of social norms, values, beliefs and socially constructed definitions.

– Normative isomorphism, where the development of norms and standards will encourage an evolution of practices. In the context of the management of innovation process, for example, we can cite the ISO 9001 standard, which includes requirements related to innovation. Documentation booklets such as FD X50-271 will guide the strategic and operational implementation of innovation in organizations (mainly small and medium enterprises [SMEs] and MSEs). The technical committee of the International Standardization Organization (ISO/TC 279) also contributes to the standardization of innovation and its management.

– Coercive isomorphism, where the evolution of the regulatory and legal framework will push organizations to change and adopt standardized practices. Management control does not seem a priori to be affected by such influences. However, the possibility for organizations to benefit from the advantages of support measures for research and development activities (such as the research tax credit) will push companies to set up tools to monitor innovation activities and the costs generated by them in order to be able to benefit from the tax advantage and obtain the documentation to justify the declarations made to the tax authorities.

In this paradigm, formal management control systems, in addition to their contribution to optimizing the performance of structures, will make it possible to display the image of a well-managed entity, pursuing rational objectives (Meyer and Rowan 1977; Covaleski et al. 1996). Management control systems are then set up and embody ideals of control and performance (Hasselbladh and Kallinikos 2000; Scott 2001; Boitier and Rivière 2011), "rationalized myths" (Hatchuel and Weil 1999). Various empirical studies have confirmed this thesis (Dillard et al. 2004; Hopper and Major 2007).

In implementing new management practices, institutions play a significant role, particularly in legitimizing these behaviors. They represent myths adopted to show that the organization conforms to external institutions.

However, these new practices do not guarantee greater efficiency of the organization. The work of Abrahamson and Rosenkopf (1993) has shown that certain practices are adopted even if they do not bring benefits, but only allow for compliance with a standard. And this tendency to mimic remains true even though the organization has information to support that it is a wrong choice (Barreto and Baden-Fuller 2006).

The authors of this work are situated in the same vein as Levinthal and March (1981), who argued that when a group of social actors adopt a behavior, it will be considered institutionalized and other social actors will be encouraged to adopt it without asking too many questions.

Different reasons will lead organizations to use similar methods, whether they are favorable and efficient. These reasons may be economic, calculative or evaluative, a quest for normative or coercive legitimacy, regulatory bodies or organizations in leadership positions, or even society. A corporate strategy is considered rational when accepted in an organizational field (DiMaggio and Powell 1983; Aldrich and Fiol 1994; Scott 1994).

Box 3.1. *The framework of neo-institutional theory (NIT)*

Organizations know they use formal, classical tools that are not necessarily adapted to their needs. They balance this framework and rigor with informal practices that complement these tools and ad hoc indicators that evolve at the same pace as the project. This is why the project will persevere even if some indicators indicate a no-go.

At this point, we could see that the intuition and experience of the actors have an essential role to play. The NIT does not apply here, and the management takes place with full awareness by the actors who are in search of a good balance of tools.

It should be noted that the organizations studied are all of a reasonable size, allowing them to allocate a specific budget to control issues. It would be interesting to study the application of the NIT in very small organizations to see if mindfulness-based management control is still applicable.

3.2.2. *A puzzle of principles and tools*

For the second question, we look at whether organizations, when making decisions in the innovation process, rely more heavily on informal practices than formal management control tools. It emerges from the case studies that informal practices take their place in managing innovation processes.

The decision-makers' intuition and experience are crucial elements in the decision-making process. Many projects would not have seen the light of day if decisions were based solely on formal tools. The trend that can be observed is the existence of political games to influence the decisions that will be taken in official instances.

The project managers and innovation directors had informal discussions in the three organizations we studied before the decision meetings. Their objective is to convince people that their project is the best one and should be allowed to continue. In this case, the persuasive skills of the project manager are more important than the indicators. Decision-making bodies are only a formality to confirm the decision to continue the project, even though they sometimes go against the indicators.

This approach is not without danger insofar as a project could be pursued because of the project manager's good argument, but it does not lead to anything.

In the same way, a project could be stopped despite its good results because the project leader was unable to convince his partners. In this context, the role of management systems is that of a safeguard (Lambert and Sponem 2009). The idea is to minimize political games, warn and make people aware of the realities, especially economic ones. As defined by the authors, we could observe a primacy of strategic thinking alongside a relatively weak impact of the power of management controllers.

The challenge for organizations is to find a balance between management control indicators and the space left for information exchange. It is essential not to fall into excesses and its dangers, which are the loss of creativity due to the omnipresence of management control tools or excessive political games due to the non-consideration of management control tools.

To characterize the implementation of management control in the context of innovation processes, we can reflect on the role of management control. Lambert and Sponem (2009) propose four functions:

– partner;

– discreet management;

– safeguard;

– omnipotent.

When the role of management controllers is that of partner, they work hand in hand with the operational staff; they respond to their requests that have a direct role to play in daily decisions. When management control is described as discreet, management control has only a weak authority, in particular to avoid hampering creativity. The management controller can also be a safeguard. Again, his authority is weak, and his client is the general management. His action may take the form of discreetly supervising the operational staff. Finally, the omnipotent function corresponds to a strong authority of the management controllers, the company's logic being very financial. The following table summarizes these four types by presenting the advantages and risks for each.

This reading grid provides a complementary vision to the control systems that organizations can implement.

	Partner	**Discreet**	**Safeguard**	**Omnipotent**
Authority	High	Low	Low	High
Client	Local	Local	MD	MD
Advantages	Consideration of the financial aspect	Managers responsible for all questions linked to their domain Creativity and reactivity promoted	Primacy of strategic thinking Training of senior managers	Systematic consideration of the financial dimension
Risks	Drift in terms of governance	Internal control Waste	Political games Waste	Short-sightedness Operational inhibition
Roles	Assistance with local decisions	Discreet verification mandate	Training of senior managers Legitimization	Centralization of power

Box 3.2. *The functions of the management controller (source: (Lambert and Sponem 2009))*

In Chapter 2, we first analyzed control management of innovation processes. Innovation, through the metaphor of the iceberg, presents a vision in two opposed blocks. The first one represents the innovation process where organizations communicate on formal tools used and practices that are widely agreed upon. The second, the submerged part of the iceberg, represents a different phenomenon since the tools and practices differ according to the organizations and can be formal or informal. Using the case studies conducted in this study, we propose a representation that goes beyond the iceberg. Indeed, the case studies have shown that the organizations studied are aware of using complementary tools to balance the weight of control on the one hand and the dangers of intuitive control on the other.

The management control systems implemented in organizations are therefore not limited to cybernetic functioning, and we adopt a broader and more extensive perspective here. The notion of puzzle has been introduced in the literature on management control to define the principles and tools used in new public management (Hood 1991; Merrien 1999; Bezes and Demazière 2011). We can apply it here to the management of the innovation process. The idea is not to highlight two opposing blocks, as the iceberg metaphor could do, but instead to highlight blocks of tools and practices that can complement one another. The notion of a puzzle seems to us to be particularly appropriate because the different bricks can fit together and thus form a more unified and homogeneous whole. However, some pieces may not be used correctly, even if they can go in the same direction. Thus, homogeneity is not assured, and an imbalance could represent a danger. Just as in the management practices of innovation processes, an excess of informality, without considering the formal bricks, can represent a danger in the continuity of projects and vice versa.

3.2.3. *An unfinished instrumentation*

We have seen that the management control systems developed in the three organizations studied, particularly at Bricolo and Fluido, are relatively recent. The innovations are disruptive, and the actors are hesitant about adopting tools and practices. The classic systems do not seem to be adapted; the actors have set up new ones that are tested and modified ad hoc. While the use of a single, isolated tool is outdated, we are not yet in the presence of a global management system covering all the dimensions proposed by Malmi and Brown (2008) (see Box 2.1) and which proposes to ensure both decision support and convergence of behaviors within the company. The tools are still limited and do not meet the expectations of all the actors, as the people interviewed in the three cases studied have shown. All three organizations are searching for relevant indicators at the right project time. Project presentation meetings, which are too time-consuming at Fluido, seem well managed at Telco. The number of projects is more significant, but the speaking time of each speaker is limited and allows for better time management. In addition to developing different tools with different practices to balance formal and informal, we cannot draw any specific managerial recommendations from this study regarding the indicators to be put in place.

SUMMARY.–

According to the iceberg representation of innovation process management, organizations have an official discourse in which the actors communicate on a rational management of innovations and in which management control tools have their place.

The reality is different, as organizations rely heavily on informal practices. Decisions are based on these practices and sometimes run counter to management control indicators. This reality is not, however, expressed at first glance by the actors.

This work led to two questions that we have studied in this chapter. The first interrogates the fact that organizations communicate a homogeneous representation of the management of innovation processes, a similar behavior, with an important use of formal management control tools that have been tested under the prism of mimicry, proposed in neo-institutional theory.

With the help of three case studies and the development of a disruptive innovation in three different organizations, Bricolo, Telco and Fluido, we understood that management control was carried out in full awareness. Indeed, even if the organizations communicate on the use of formal tools and a control intended to be rational, they also use informal practices and are aware that they are seeking a balance between the different practices. Organizations are not fooled and do not seek to imitate at all costs practices that are useful in other contexts. They know that management control is necessary for any development and that finding the right indicators and monitoring rhythm is challenging.

The second question examines whether organizations rely more heavily on informal practices than formal management control tools when making decisions in the innovation process. Indeed, we have observed that many decisions were taken against the results of the indicators proposed by the management control tools. We noted that intuitive control was present in the context of innovations and that if the actors "believed" in the development of the product, this was favorable to its continuity.

Once again, the actors comply consciously, using management control tools as safeguards according to the definition proposed by Lambert and Sponem (2009). The different practices combine like a puzzle and the important thing is to find a balance between formal control, whose excesses can inhibit creativity and informal practices that can lead to power plays that can be harmful.

The management control practices of innovation processes do not appear complete and require further research, which could be directed, for example, in a similar context with organizations that recurrently develop disruptive innovations or in another context where management control would also be in tension. In the latter case, it would be a matter of studying the balance found by management control.

4

Management Control in a Specific Environment, the Case of the Social and Solidarity Economy

Following Chapter 3, we realized that innovation management was an unfinished business. Organizations do not yet have the tools and best practices.

In this chapter, we explore other organizations where management control is in tension. We focus more specifically on the case of the social and solidarity economy (SSE), where management control is in tension on the one hand with the need to innovate and on the other hand with strong human and social values. Indeed, the social and solidarity economy organizations evolve in a rapidly changing environment. Funders favor innovative organizations that offer solutions at lower costs while guaranteeing the quality of the service provided. The SSE structures are therefore characterized by:

– the need to innovate to propose new solutions;

– the ambition to develop projects with human-centered solid values;

– the need to guarantee a financial balance to ensure the sustainability of the projects.

First of all, management control is in conflict with innovation. Indeed, control and creativity appear as opposites with objectives that seem contradictory. Then, management control is in tension with strong social and solidarity values. Indeed, these are the priority of the actors who may consider financial issues non-priority issues.

Our objective is to understand how SSE actors deal with these two levels of tension and what the inspirations are that can inspire other organizations where management control is in tension.

In the first section, we will discuss the context of the SSE and the place occupied by management control tools. In the second section, we will see the role of the organization with the case study of the Apprentis d'Auteuil Foundation, which has implemented a new management tool. Finally, in the last section, we will look at a new way of managing: informal, values-based management.

4.1. The context of social economy organizations and their management

After presenting the context of social and solidarity economy organizations and having studied the place of management control tools within this sector of activity, we will meet with six SSE structures to learn more about the place of management control in these organizations and how they deal with the tensions defined above.

4.1.1. *The context of social and solidarity economy organizations*

This is a relatively recent sector of activity, which emerged in the 1970s. This sector now plays a significant role in today's economy, accounting for 10% of GDP in Europe. Since the promulgation of the law on SSE in July 2014, it is recognized as a specific innovative and sustainable mode of undertaking and brings together establishments from different fields of activity. The principles defined therein are an economy of requirement based on the values of democratic and participatory governance, limited profitability and social utility. These structures' internal functioning and activities are based on a principle of solidarity, with people at the heart of the organization. The service rendered is privileged over the profit made, and the social dimension is integrated into economic life (Ceges: *Conseil des entreprises, employeurs et groupements de l'économie sociale*).

These SSE organizations are currently evolving in a changing environment. The economic context is at the forefront of these changes. Often financed by private and public resources, the latter are being restricted, and the budgets allocated to the operation of the institutions' services are being impacted. The financial difficulties of public funding bodies are leading to increased competition between the various players in this sector of activity, particularly *through* the democratization of call procedures for projects and call for tenders procedures, which encourage the structures to propose innovative solutions. For example, in the medico-social sector, the law on hospitals, patients, health and territories, promulgated on 21 July 2009, reserves part of the calls for projects for experimental and innovative projects. The creative character of projects from SSE entrepreneurs is also promoted by funding support mechanisms such as the European Social Fund (ESF). Frédéric Deck, President of the Regional Chamber of Social and Solidarity Economy (CRESS 2013), considers that "the ESF and the SSE make a common cause for innovation in the territories".

At the same time, it is important to note the current societal changes (notably the increase in precariousness and poverty), which open up new development opportunities for organizations. Richez-Battesti et al. (2012) point out that the scale of the current crisis is encouraging a renewed interest in innovation, which is supposed to be the source of a new growth regime.

Intensified competition, a fragile economic balance and a changing and growing demand require structures to adapt. They need to propose new solutions that meet the needs of society while respecting the constrained budget imposed by public finances.

The SSE structures are thus characterized by:

– the need to innovate and to propose new solutions;

– the ambition to develop projects with strong human values;

– the need to guarantee a financial balance to ensure the sustainability of the projects.

Given these characteristics, management control faces significant challenges in terms of performance measurement. Indeed, it is necessary to have tools that allow the control of the different variables that will guarantee the financial balance and quality of services as well as their coherence with the organization's values, and all this without inhibiting the birth of new ideas. One of the management imperatives will ensure that the projects do not deviate from their primary ambitions (social and solidarity values).

4.1.2. *The place of management control tools in the social and solidarity economy*

In the current context, where SSE organizations have to meet their funders' requirements and have a strategic will to develop, management tools naturally find their place. Indeed, management control can facilitate coherence between strategy and concrete, daily actions (Bouquin 2008). The tools act as an interface between management, which communicates goals and allocates resources, and operations, which manages day-to-day activities.

However, the SSE is characterized by social and solidarity values that are intrinsic to the organizations and prevalent in their daily lives. The question of the management of these organizations raises questions for researchers. Indeed, the values defended by these structures and their limited lucrativeness seem to go against the objectives of management tools, which are often synonymous with maximizing profit and organizational performance. In fact, control tools are defined as the means to measure performance.

In the context of the SSE, where profitability is limited and where the consideration of social and solidarity values is the foundation of the organizations, it is important to try to define the term performance. Forbes (1998) and Herman and Renz (1999) point out the difficulties in understanding this notion in the non-profit sector. This is confirmed by Kaplan (2001), who explains that although organizations "must certainly manage their spending and adhere to financial budgets, their success cannot be measured by how much they spend within the budget, even if spending is kept well below budget". Bourguignon (1995) gives a rather broad view:

> In management, performance is the achievement of organizational goals.

This definition implies that objectives may have been defined before the action and that these are not necessarily linked to economic profitability. The SSE sector is characterized by different types of ambitions. Löning et al. (2003) refer to this diversity of sometimes conflicting objectives that make performance measurement complex.

Different authors have noted this ambiguity, and divergent approaches to the issue of managing these structures are found in the literature (Bidet 2003; Laville and Glémain 2009; Codello-Guijarro and Béji-Bécheur 2015).

Thus, to avoid going against social objectives and maintain the "natural performance of informal organizations that they like to cultivate" (Valéau 2003, p. 9), some reject the implementation of management tools. As these tools embody classic profitability objectives, they clash with the values defended by this economy, which places the human and the social above financial considerations. However, this resistance to the development of management tools presents a risk of losing competitiveness and performance. Indeed, the democratization of the call for projects and tenders procedures, as well as the generalization, in the medico-social sector, of multi-year contracts of objectives and means (*contrats pluriannuels d'objectifs et de moyens*, CPOM) with the regional health agency (*agence régionale de santé*, ARS) and the department, generate increased competition between the different actors in this sector of activity and oblige organizations to have fine management of their activities. In addition, SSE organizations are often financed by private and public resources, which tend to decrease, and the budgets granted to establishments are impacted.

This intensification of competition and a fragile economic balance lead some organizations to acquire management tools. Capron (2012) presents these structures, above all as firms, with specificities due to their status. From this point of view, like organizations in traditional sectors, they must be managed, and since "one only manages well what one measures" (Berland et al. 2008), they adopt management monitoring to track their results and performance. As a result of institutional isomorphism (DiMaggio and Powell 1983), these tools are often derived from traditional sectors (Beji-Becheur et al. 2008). For Enjolras (1998) and Bidet (2003), institutional isomorphism obeys, in the case of associations, three types of isomorphism:

– normative through the professionalization of the sector;

– coercive due to the influence of funders;

– mimetic because there is a recourse to proven solutions to the given problems.

These organizations "are increasingly importing managerial techniques from companies" (Boussard 2008, p. 12). Laville (2009) refers to this phenomenon of "managerialism" which consists of applying management to new domains and which can be defined as a "system of description, explanation and interpretation of the world based on management categories" (Chanlat 1998).

Although it responds to the changes in this sector of activity, this trend again represents a risk for these structures, that of losing their specificities due to their sector. Indeed, the classic tools do not carry the values of the SSE and are, therefore, difficult to adopt. Meyer and Ohana (2007) and Vatteville (2006) have highlighted that tools based on monetary incentives or specific accounting standards will run counter to the principle of solidarity that lies at the heart of the values of these structures. Demoustier (2002, p. 105) considers the introduction of these tools "not [as] a betrayal, but [as] an adjustment to the environment". The tools are therefore necessary for certain structures to support their development, but they risk contradicting their intrinsic values. This pitfall is not negligible, and it is important to consider it. Grimes (2010) studied the impact of performance measurement tools on organizations' identity in the social sector.

In addition to measuring performance, management tools allow us to know who we are, to give meaning to our actions and to build the identity of organizations. Beyond their explicit functions, management tools have political and structural effects (Gilbert 1998). Waggoner et al. (1999), Townley et al. (2003) and Henri (2006) define performance measurement tools as an example of the values shared within the structure. It is understandable that if one applies the management tools of for-profit organizations directly to the SSE sector, where the values are different, these risk are lost. For Méda (2000, p. 94):

> There is a good chance [...] that the projects developed by the social economy, cooperatives and/or associations [...] will, as soon as they offer an interesting profitability, be taken over by classic companies, by the famous market.

These tensions between control and social values result from the fact that they are hybrid organizations that are subject to several institutional logics (Battilana 2010). These clash (Bovais 2014) in organizations that alternately choose one or the other.

A last stream of literature, in which we place ourselves, reconciles these two opposing institutional logics by proposing the use of hybrid tools that balance the need for control with the need to take into account the values of the organization (Hollandts 2009; Acquier et al. 2011; Bayle and Dupuis 2012; Demoustier and Malo 2012; André 2015; Château-Terrisse 2015). This is a response to Moisdon (2005, p. 249), who calls for "other models that would make management tools not vectors of conformation and standardization, but openings to spaces of freedom and collective creation".

Management control is not a classic tool but a set of mechanisms and processes that guarantee coherence between strategy and concrete, daily actions (Bouquin 2008). This strategy can:

– be different from performance objectives specific to for-profit organizations;

– contain social objectives as for SSE organizations;

– enable the reconciliation of democratic functioning and economic success (Ghent 2015).

4.1.3. *Management between control and creativity*

To better understand the concrete practices of organizations in this sector, we studied six structures through a qualitative study in the form of interviews (Abrapa, Adapei, Apprentis d'Auteuil, Mutuelle française d'Alsace, Scoprobat and Sonnenhof). We wanted to learn more about the place of management control in these structures:

– to understand the structure and missions of management control departments;

– to know the nature and use of tools;

– to know the upcoming developments in management control tools.

To obtain reliable and representative data, special attention was paid to sample selection. For high quality, the sample must have dissimilarities and similitude points (Rubin and Rubin 2005).

In our case study, the differences are found in the fields of action of the different structures and the common points are embodied in the social and solidarity values of each of them.

Table 4.1 presents the characteristics of the six organizations studied.

	Type of structure	Main fields of action	Number of people helped	Description
Abrapa	Association	Help and services	20,000 people helped in the Bas-Rhin	Abrapa has existed for 53 years, has 3,000 employees spread over various sites and has a turnover of 100 million euros. The services offered include assistance and support at home, the association's core business, day care centers, hospitals, retirement homes, etc.
Adapei	Association	Help for people with mental disabilities	1,000 people welcomed in the Bas-Rhin	Adapei (Association of parents and friends of mentally handicapped persons) has a recognized mission of public utility. It has 23 establishments of different types: specialized homes, medicalized homes, specialized homes, establishments and services for assistance through work and adapted companies.
Apprentis d'Auteuil	Foundation	Child protection training for integration	23,000 young people with educational, social or family problems are being taken care of in France, including 754 in the Alsace region	Apprentis d'Auteuil is recognized as being of public utility. Its mission is "to give confidence and hope to young people in difficulty and to help them build their life project, and to support vulnerable families in their educational responsibilities". Apprentis d'Auteuil has been established in France for nearly 150 years and offers various services: accommodation, training, reception without accommodation, and integration.

	Type of structure	Main fields of action	Number of people helped	Description
Mutuelle française d'Alsace	Mutual insurance	Health care supply: access to care for all	727,000 members protected by mutual insurance companies in Alsace	The Mutualité française d'Alsace federates more than 200 mutual insurance companies and represents the interests of the members of the mutual insurance companies. It also offers various services via various mutualist care areas spread throughout the region. The services offered are: – dental centers (8) – optical centers (11) – hearing centers (10)
Scoprobat	Production cooperative (Scop)	Insertion	58 employees integrated on the different sites	Scoprobat is an insertion scop that gathers three entities: Batiscop, Scoproxim and Proximpoint Lavender. They were three companies that merged in 2012 to form a scop.
Sonnenhof	Foundation	Help for people with disabilities	1,200 people cared for in the Alsace region	This structure, recognized as public utility, has been working for more than 125 years. It has 23 establishments grouped under four hubs: – juniors; – social and professional integration; – specialized reception for adults; – seniors. The reception structures are diversified. They are medical-educational institutes, accommodation homes, establishments and services for assistance through work, specialized homes and hostels, retirement homes or even vacation centers.

Table 4.1. *Characteristics of the organizations studied*

The interviews were conducted based on an interview guide that covered the organization of the management control department, the characteristics of the management tools and their evolution.

One to two hours per interview were necessary to obtain the different information. The people interviewed were controllers or members of the management.

4.1.3.1. *The structure and missions of the management control departments*

The interviews revealed that, in general, management control departments are relatively modest in size, with one or two people. The missions of all the management controllers interviewed are based on the same themes:

– analysis and dissemination of information;

– advice and warning;

– production of various financial statements for internal or external stakeholders.

The missions of SSE management controllers are similar to the main roles defined by Chiapello (1990): technician, consultant-evaluator and advisor.

4.1.3.2. *The nature and use of the tools*

We mainly find tools with standard formats for each structure's establishments, but which can be differentiated according to the recipients (management or operational). It is often a simple spreadsheet listing the accounts with budget variances. On the other hand, if the level of detail is at the account level, analyses are carried out on the large mass level, with a specific focus on payroll, activity levels and purchasing.

Interactivity is absent from the tool. The tool is used as a support, often sent by email. When communicating by email, very little interactivity is observed. Due to a lack of time, the recipient sometimes does not even open the table. More important interactivity is to be noted when the management controller takes the time to meet individually with each stakeholder. This is an opportunity to present the figures and variances, and thus to understand the differences and consider action plans in the event of deviation. In addition to disseminating information, it is also an opportunity to raise awareness of the figures.

4.1.3.3. *The evolving nature of the tools*

Finally, an important point to note is the evolving nature of the management tools for all the structures. Indeed, they have all recently implemented voluntary innovations in their management tools, and each is considering further improvements. These improvements can be linked to the need for the organizations to offer innovative services, and we can then ask ourselves what links there may be between the creativity observed in the control systems implemented and the creativity expected in terms of the services offered in this SSE sector. The areas of improvement envisaged include more precise monitoring of certain charges and a tool that provides greater assistance in decision-making, particularly by promoting interactivity.

In the case of the Apprentis d'Auteuil Foundation, for example, we have recently implemented a new management control tool. We note an expression of creativity in the nature of the management tool. This tool is intended to be simple, intuitive and accessible to all players. Each establishment has one tool customized according to the needs of the various stakeholders (establishment directors, support functions, head office) who have chosen the most appropriate indicators. The choice of customization was made because of the heterogeneity of the establishments in the territory and brought a particular character to the way of measuring the performance of each structure. The tools developed are intended to be scalable according to the needs of the facilities but also to the environment. The following section examines in greater detail the process of building this new management tool and the organization's role in this project.

NOTE.– In the particular sector of the SSE characterized by its strong values, the search for financial balance and the need to innovate, we have noted, through the study of different structures, the evolving nature of the management tools used with the integration of voluntary and recent innovations. The objective of this common dynamic is to adapt the performance measurement tools to the sector's specific needs.

We therefore find innovations within management control, notably *through* adapting management tools. Nevertheless, it appears that management tools are not yet able to evaluate the performance of the innovation process.

4.2. Organizational innovation as a key to resolving tensions

This section is dedicated to the study of the construction of a new management tool, and we more specifically study the case of the Apprentis d'Auteuil Foundation.

4.2.1. *The influence of the measurement*

Despite the difficulties that may arise, it is in the interest of organizations to consider the different objectives and integrate them into management tools. Indeed, Grimes (2010) studied, in the social sector, the impact that performance measurement tools could have on the identity of organizations: the management tool allows, in addition to measuring performance, to know who one is, to give meaning to action and to build the identity of organizations. For Plantz et al. (1997) and Kaplan (2001), measuring performance are real tools for communicating the identity of the structure, its missions and its strategy. Waggoner et al. (1999), Townley et al. (2003) and Henri (2006) even define performance measurement tools as an example of the values shared within the organization. They are used to communicate within and outside the organization. Studies have shown that these tools induce organizational change, and organizations strive to become what they measure (Grimes 2010). Light (2000) compares management tools in the social economy sector to a compass that should be followed.

Thus, we can realize that it is necessary to set objectives, to be able to measure them so that they take part in the construction of organizational identity. The specificity of SSE structures compared to the traditional market sector is characterized by the strong adherence to certain values. This distinctive feature should be reflected in the management control tools.

In the particular case of the social economy, Grimes (2010) has highlighted the influence of funders on the definition of the organizational identities of funded structures through the imposed performance measurement methods. The indicators defined become the guidelines for partnerships within this sector of activity (Grimes 2010). The organizational identity that the funded structure creates for itself is induced by the tools imposed by the funders.

The formats of these reports are more or less standardized, and it is understandable that given the influence on the identity of organizations, if the funder favors standardization, this will invariably impact the characteristics of organizations by creating more homogeneity in the sector of activity.

4.2.2. *The case of Apprentis d'Auteuil: the role of the organization in the construction of a new management tool*

4.2.2.1. *Presentation of the case*

Apprentis d'Auteuil, a foundation recognized as being of public utility, works in prevention and protection of children. A foundation is a private organization that aims to pursue work of general interest. It must be non-profit, have unbiased management and not benefit only a restricted circle of people. It is defined by article 18 of law No. 87-571 of 23 July 1987 on the development of sponsorship as "the act by which one or more natural or legal persons decide to irrevocably allocate goods, rights or resources to the realization of a work of general interest and not for profit".

Apprentis d'Auteuil is present in France, with 230 establishments (accommodation, training and support) and 5,500 employees. It is also developing a network of partners in 50 countries where 27,000 young people and 5,500 families are supported. In France, the foundation is organized into regions, which are divided into territories, each with a management team with support functions. Our study was conducted in the eastern region, which includes all the establishments in Alsace and the Ardennes. This area is particularly interesting because it brings together establishments of very different natures (children's homes, daycare, training establishments, crèches, integration assistance). This plurality of organizations and therefore of missions underlies the need for different monitoring indicators. Faced with divergent expectations, a need to adapt the tool has arisen, which is why the tools created are highly personalized. The translation framework is therefore relevant because it allows the needs of each of the organization's actors to be considered.

> The fact that the actors are aware of and interested in the subject is insufficient to invest them in the project. Chemin and Gilbert (2010, p. 77), who have worked on the effect of importing management tools from the market sector into the SSE, have highlighted the importance of the interplay of actors in this sector during the implementation of management tools:
>
>> The construction of the evaluation would imply taking into account all the actors whose values we wish to integrate into the act of intervention. Otherwise, those who embody the funder are the only ones to play the game, to the detriment of civil society [...] The problem is therefore to manage to associate the different spheres in a plural governance.
>
> The translation framework makes it possible to support the construction of a management tool in the SSE by involving the actors to minimize the upheaval of this introduction (Agro et al. 1996). The theory of translation (Latour and Woolgar 1979; Callon 1981; Callon 1986; Latour 1987) proposes to consider the interests of the different stakeholders and thus encourage mobilization and synergy in the long term around the project. The translation represents a set of "negotiations, intrigues, acts of persuasion, calculations, violence" (Callon and Latour

2006). The construction results from discussions, consensus and power relations between the different parties. Exchanges or "moments" (Callon 1986) must be provoked and encouraged to bring out the needs of the stakeholders to be assembled and transcribed. Dreveton and Rocher (2010) couple the translation framework with the definition of a construction process of a management tool studied in a French region, from the inventory of existing tools and practices to the implementation of the tool in the organization. We have reproduced and pre-presented this framework in Figure 4.1. The authors emphasize that the various actors' active participation throughout the process guarantees success. Other authors have also used translation in the construction of management tools (Lemaire 2013; Nobre and Zawadzki 2013; Perray-Redslob and Malaurent 2015).

Box 4.1. *The framework of translation*

The construction of a new management tool in this area replaces the tool that has been in place for several years. The dashboard format is similar to those used in for-profit organizations and was not used by the directors of establishments (DEs) in their decisions. On the one hand, this tool was not a basis for dialogue between the players, and on the other, although it presented financial indicators, the DEs often expressed the need to "know their figures". The main interests of a new tool were therefore the establishment of a regular and constructive dialogue between the DEs and the management control department, as well as assistance in the management of the structures with the provision of information allowing the financial data of the institutions to be understood. The existing tool did not meet these needs and, above all, did not consider the specificities of the SSE. We can see that the integration of a traditional tool, without adaptation, is not pertinent and is not used at Apprentis d'Auteuil. We are planning the construction and implementation of the new management tool according to the issues it must address.

Increased competition, professionalization in the SSE and the size of Apprentis d'Auteuil have generated a need for management for the structure's directors. The foundation is in a cost-killing perspective, a constant search for savings on operating budgets to meet the objectives imposed by the funders. This method can be compared to the practices of many profit-making companies that have developed tools to track down extra expenses. Although the problem seems to be the same, interviews with DEs about the tools in place at the beginning of our intervention showed that they were of little relevance and not used for decision-making. The fundamental difference between a cost reduction program in the SSE and a traditional sector comes from the different objectives of this method. In one case, it will allow, in addition to the efficient use of available resources, to invest more in programs with important social and solidarity values. In contrast, in the other case, the reductions will allow for better shareholders' remuneration. The organization needs to communicate to the stakeholders (in our case, the DEs) about these management and cost reduction objectives. It is, therefore, not only a question of reducing operating expenses, but also of obtaining more resources to invest in new projects serving the organization's values. The aim is to make DEs, who are disinclined to use management control figures in their operational decisions, aware that these figures can benefit the cause they are defending. With this in mind, during the development of the tool, the regional management of Apprentis d'Auteuil and the support functions conveyed this message to the DEs who did not use the tools previously in place. The attention of the actors was therefore solicited throughout the process of the construction of the management tool, from the identification of shortcomings to the dissemination and use of the tool. This was done through formal or informal communication, unplanned interactions and personalized encouragement or advice. These are all means of promoting awareness of the benefits of equipping the organization and gaining acceptance of a logic of control coupled with social values. These exchanges are also the moment to collaborate around the tool and thus adapt it to be as close as possible to the needs of the different actors. We have noted significant differences in the acceptance and use of the tool depending on the actors. Thus, for the support functions of the territorial management and some DEs who were already sensitive to management issues, the tool was distributed naturally, with little reluctance. On the other hand, for other DEs, the dissemination and use of the new tool were more complex. Resistance to the figures was felt. With the help of informal practices such as encouragement, appropriate advice, the assurance that their needs would be taken into account and the possibility of modifying the tool further, the tool was accepted.

4.2.2.2. The construction of a tool appropriate to the needs and interests of the various stakeholders

The second challenge for Apprentis d'Auteuil is to build a tool that is truly appropriate to the values that the different actors defend. We have seen that using a traditional tool does not allow us to respond to this. Important work on the knowledge of the needs of each actor, recipients of the tool, with 18 interviews and a survey allowed understanding them better. The interviews were transcribed and then analyzed thematically. The objective was to identify the different respondents' contradictions, similarities, nuances and particularities. The analysis of the needs of the various actors (DEs, support functions) showed that expectations were different depending on the respondent's profession, as shown in Table 4.2.

Trades	Expectations
Establishment's directors	Simple indicators that allow for operational decisions Interactive zone allows exchanges with the management control on the meaning of certain indicators
Management control department	Detailed analysis of each structure to understand the ins and outs of certain figures to advise the DE in their decision making
Territorial management	Synthetic indicators that provide a quick and global view of the situation of an institution

Table 4.2. *The main expectations of the different actors*

To meet these very different expectations and to have a tool that is relevant and used by the different categories of actors, the tool adopted is built according to different layers. Figure 4.1 presents the architecture of the tool that has been implemented.

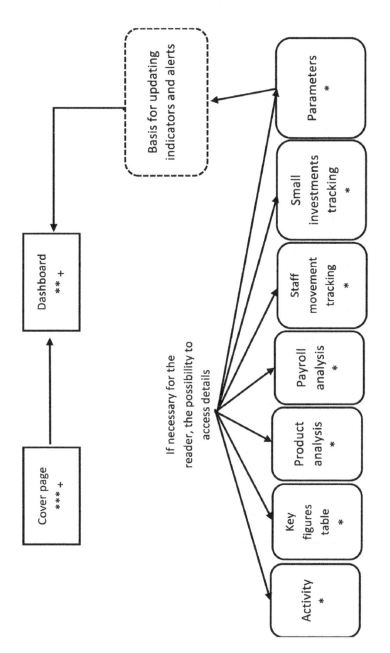

Figure 4.1A. *Architecture of the implemented tool*

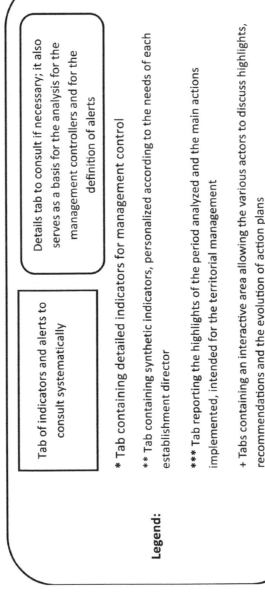

Tab of indicators and alerts to consult systematically

Details tab to consult if necessary; it also serves as a basis for the analysis for the management controllers and for the definition of alerts

Legend:

* Tab containing detailed indicators for management control

** Tab containing synthetic indicators, personalized according to the needs of each establishment director

*** Tab reporting the highlights of the period analyzed and the main actions implemented, intended for the territorial management

+ Tabs containing an interactive area allowing the various actors to discuss highlights, recommendations and the evolution of action plans

Figure 4.1B. *Architecture of the implemented tool (continued)*

In addition to adapting to needs through the different strata, significant customization was made in the tab entitled "your dashboard" (Figure 4.1). This tab, intended for DEs, contains indicators they have chosen and adapted to their institution. It contains different parts: the level of activity, a very important indicator because the activity directly affects the subsidies that can be received by public funders; human resources, the main expense item for establishments in this sector; other expenses and income.

Each part is composed of the indicators deemed most relevant by the DE. For example, an indicator for the collection of receivables for a private school is necessary for the DE because actions are taken to improve the collection of receivables. The possibility of having a follow-up indicator makes it possible to measure the efforts made. Another example concerns a residential facility for which an indicator reflecting the facility's occupancy rate has been added. In the section on indicators of the institution's expenses and income, we find the indicators most closely linked to the specificities of the SSE.

In fact, in the other expenses, the flexibility of the DEs is important, and we find indicators specific to the activities carried out, such as outings with children and/or discovery classes. The same is true for revenues: in addition to the fees that depend on the activity, other revenues can be received by the establishments, such as donations, sponsorship, charity sales or activity-specific actions that the DEs can manage.

The presentation format of the indicators is varied: graphics, simple indicators and/or conditional formatting. They are built from the information obtained in the additional tabs and are automatically updated. The interactivity zones also show the strong customization of the tool. They make it possible to account for and formalize each person's work, as well as the questions and/or areas of improvement envisaged to explain or improve certain indicators. Because of the diversity of the institutions in our case study panel, customization was necessary to produce relevant tools.

The construction required a lot of back and forth between the DEs and the management control department to understand the expectations and obtain indicators that were as close as possible to the expectations and that could be constructed with the information in the information system. This iterative process is shown in Figure 4.2, which highlights the back-and-forth process as it progresses.

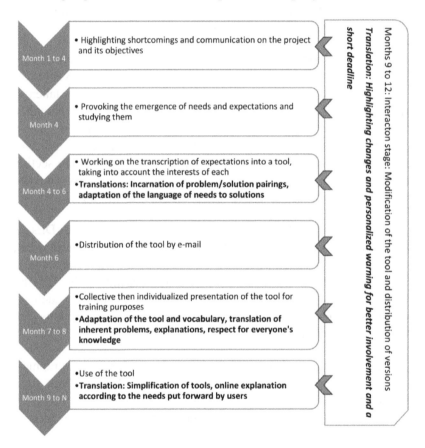

Figure 4.2. *Steps in the tool building process*

4.2.2.3. *The role of management control tools*

Faced with a new economic environment and the need to set up a management system for the establishments, Apprentis d'Auteuil has developed a new management control tool that is better adapted to the needs of the players. As we have already mentioned, Bouquin (2008) has highlighted the role of management control as an interface between strategic control on the one hand and operational control on the other. The tool set up at Apprentis d'Auteuil allows for this interface role. Indeed, the organization's management can communicate its objectives to the various directors of the establishments, who can follow up via indicators co-constructed with management control based on translation theory. As we have seen, the objective is to ensure the best support service with the lowest cost, within a cost-killing perspective, and the indicators have been constructed with this in mind.

Management tools find their place in SSE organizations, which are currently changing, and are involved in the modernization of the management information system. It is an essential element in the management process and a fundamental component of management control. In fact, the latter contributes to the development of the management information system by providing performance evaluation benchmarks that help to organize the accounting system and to draw up management charts (Teller 1999). The management information system produces information and indicators to ensure the management of the company's activities. It automates and facilitates the administrative processes and the conduction of activities, and is thus aimed at all the company's users: operational actors, managers and executives.

4.2.2.4. *The influence of the organization*

This line of thought on the organization's real roles in implementing a management tool refers essentially to the theory of attention (Ocasio 1997). This theory can help reconcile democratic functioning and economic success (Ghent 2015).

In the case study of the Apprentis d'Auteuil Foundation, we noted that the actors did not use a traditional tool. It was only by taking into account the needs and interests of each of them, including those related to their social missions, that a new tool that would be accepted and used could be proposed. The need for control is not a priority for the actors, and the theory of attention proposes to make them aware that it is an important element for the good management of the institution and thus encourages the implementation and acceptance of a management tool.

Attention theory (Ocasio 1997) relates the behavior of firms in channeling and distributing attention to the choices that decision-makers make. The links between individual information processes and behavior in the structure are made explicit. Attention is defined as the behavior of an individual who devotes limited time and effort to one item over others (Ocasio 1997). Attentional selection occurs when the individual's act is voluntary and induces different actions. The involvement of the organization is highlighted in the selection of attention. How the organization distributes and controls the allocation of problem-solution pairs will influence individuals (Ocasio 2011). Mayer (2016) shows that so-called issue-selling practices can influence actors' attention (Dutton et al. 2001). In this case, like the attention approach, different action levers are available to the organization:

– the rules, procedures and communication channels that it puts in place: it will therefore be necessary to communicate in formats that have a strong impact on the issues to be addressed as a priority;

– interaction with others: the organization can act by promoting meeting moments to exchange and convey information;

– the embodiment of problem and solution pairs in symbols, ideas and values of the organization: it will be a question of conveying the corporate culture and drawing a parallel with current or past problems;

– past actions, projects and decisions taken by the organization: it may be interesting to publicize and communicate on those that the organization wishes to use as an example.

The theory of attention can be related to our field of study, which is interested in constructing a management tool in the SSE. The actors, who take decisions, are represented by the managers who are at origin of operational decisions. The selectivity of attention takes on its full meaning insofar as these individuals have an enormous number of requests to which they must respond in a limited time. They have to prioritize their activities and, in the case of the SSE, these activities are more related to the social mission of the structure. The choice to give more or less importance to one subject compared to another is conditioned by different parameters where the organization plays a predominant role through different channels. First, official and personal communication influences the actors by setting objectives. In this way, the focus can be on different medium- and short-term orientations. In the SSE, social objectives are a priority despite the increasing importance of the economic model. They are communicated by management and are strong levers for the organization to direct the attention and actions of decision-makers. For example, in the more specific child protection sector, the Apprentis d'Auteuil Foundation conveys strong values of benevolence and trust. These values are intended for the various actors who take charge of this mission and implement it via the institution of exchanges of attentive and benevolent listening that will contribute to the safety and well-being of a child. Then come to the interactions with peers; decision-makers will communicate about their actions, challenges, successes and failures, thereby contributing to shifting attention. If the organization of the SSE manages to communicate the interests of managing the social objectives of the structure with some of the actors, the latter can become representative of this notion with their colleagues. This influence can then be used in the form of a success story to promote interest in the creation of a management tool.

Box 4.2. *The theory of attention (source: Ocasio 1997)*

Valéau (2003) has shown that organizations with limited profitability rely heavily on informality. In the case of the Apprentis d'Auteuil, we have chosen to use this asset and solicit the attention of the actors in particular by using informal communications. It is therefore the consideration of attention and its fluctuations, and the emergence of expectations and needs that, once translated, led to the creation of a functional tool in line with everyone's interests and which is used without reluctance. This long process is subject to various stages, each of which has been the subject of special attention in order to personalize the tool and its use. Interaction, especially informal interaction, accompanied by a good understanding of the actors' problems and by showing empathy, was an important element in the acceptance of the tool. It was necessary to use a major communication channel to attract the attention of stakeholders and to focus on priority issues. It is also important, from the outset of the process, to highlight the shortcomings of the existing tools for good management and to communicate widely about the project, its interests and its objectives.

The meetings with the DEs allowed the emergence of needs and expectations which, in a second stage, were the subject of a study. This stage resulted in the embodiment of the pairs of problems and solutions. It was the way in which the organization distributed and controlled the allocation of these pairs that influenced the individuals (Ocasio 1997). Our work of transcribing expectations into a tool that takes everyone's interests into account then took place. All of these variables influence adherence to the project.

Progress in the implementation of the tool also depends on the active participation and knowledge of the individuals involved in the project. It was, therefore, essential for the organization to provide regular reminders, to provoke "moments" in the sense meant by Callon (1981), to make the different actors aware of the importance of their participation. This made it possible to adapt the tool, translate the inherent problems and put forward explanations. These changes, which are sources of disruption (Agro et al. 1996), had to be accompanied and were the subject of encouragement and adapted advice within a short period to avoid any form of discouragement. At this stage, the pre-presentation of the tool adapted to each user, the possible modifications of the tool and the dissemination of improved versions constituted a turning point before it could be simplified according to the needs of each user for its final use.

The selectivity of the attention could be observed, from the beginning, but also throughout the project. Indeed, a reminder, often informal, was regularly necessary to remind the various stakeholders of the project's existence and the opportunity to participate in it. The means of communication were a variable that made it possible to influence the choice of issues addressed by the individuals. For example, the email distribution of the dashboard did not allow its implementation, but meetings were necessary, and their impact was greater than for the first communication format. These meetings with each stakeholder made it possible to take into account each person's needs, doubts and questions and train them to use the tool. As the institutions are all different and their management skills vary according to their profiles, there was a real added value in personalizing each of these exchanges.

The absence of a hierarchical link between the management controllers who initiated the project, and the actors did not allow for a very significant influence on the rules and procedures variable. It could have been enhanced by the intervention of the line manager, who could have encouraged the individuals through the annual interviews by setting objectives for economic balance. The corporate culture, strongly anchored within the foundation, favors a priority selection of issues dealing with the quality of care for young people and naturally minimizes the question of economic follow-up.

The organization did have a role in influencing individuals' choices regarding selecting one issue over another. The different variables proposed by Ocasio (1997) could be reflected in the field of study, with each variable influencing project adherence to a greater or lesser extent.

Attention theory is particularly useful in the context of the SSE because it allows us to deal with the natural tensions between management control and the more social and solidarity-based operational objectives, particularly through reminders of the project's objectives and interests. Different variables are available to the organization to influence the work group and communicate the interest and importance of management control in this sector. Through the analysis of our case, personalized communications are a strong vector in the influence of individuals. The use of informal communication, made possible by the geographical proximity of the different actors, was an asset in the construction of this new tool and particularly adapted to the SSE sector (Valéau 2003).

Another element, which is important and reflected in the case studied, is the need for the organization not to rush the actors in its communication in the interest of using management tools. It was important to give them time to mature the idea. This is why, after informal communications, the implementation of a questionnaire to analyze the needs of each actor allowed them to think about the idea of a new tool and take the time to question themselves pragmatically about its use.

4.2.2.5. *The importance of the role of actors*

Berland et al. (2008) have emphasized that "we only manage well what we measure"; we can complete this sentence by saying that we only manage well what we measure "with quality", that is, with indicators resulting from a process of co-construction. Measurement can be defined in this context as quantification, which is a prerequisite for measurement, since it "authorizes" the measurement of certain phenomena (Desrosières 2008, p. 10). Measurement can be based on realistic metalogies or, as in the social sciences, on a more or less complex set of conventions. In the case of Apprentis d'Auteuil, before the implementation of a new tool, measurement indicators that might seem relevant to certain actors were proposed, for example, the management control department. But these indicators were not used by the DEs, who were the decision-makers and actors of the economic balance of their structure. They were therefore not relevant, and the tool did not fulfil its role.

In practice, an effort has been made to integrate the various actors in the process of construction, and implementation process was observed. One of the first steps was to communicate the interest of the project following the shortcomings that could be observed. Interest was thus aroused among the DEs, and it was then that the first questionnaire to study the needs was distributed. Faced with structures of very different natures, the choice was made to propose a personalized tool to correspond as closely as possible to the expectations of each. This desire to produce a dashboard closer to expectations had the objective of increasing involvement leading to a better use rate. The evolution of the motivation of the DEs at different stages of the project is shown in Table 4.3. This subjective indicator was obtained by taking into account the following parameters:

– the speed of response to requests;

– the number of questions raised by the project;

– the number of suggestions made by DEs;

– responses to questionnaires regarding interest in the tool.

Temporalities	Steps	DE motivation
Months 1–4	Highlighting deficiencies and communicating the project and its objectives	↗
Month 4	To provoke the emergence of needs and expectations and to study them	↗↗
Months 4–6	Work on transcribing expectations into a tool, taking into account the interests of each person	↘↘
Month 6	Distribution of the tool by email	→
Months 7–8	Group and individual presentation of the tool for training purposes	↗↗
Months 9–12	Modification of the tool and release of improved versions	↗
Month 12 to...	Use of the tool	→

Table 4.3. *Stages of the process and motivation of DEs*

Even though the tool was built using a participatory approach that took into account the needs of the individuals, there were sometimes strong fluctuations in motivation and investment. These variations can be linked to the duration of the different stages as well as to the habits of the operational actors, that is, to the low involvement in management issues. Taking the time to explain the management issues, the shortcomings observed, then questioning the various stakeholders about their expectations and needs, and finally, in a third phase, explaining the tool, its use and how it responds to expectations helped to launch a positive dynamic.

To keep this course and guarantee the use of the tool over the long term, work is undeniable. For example, imagine regular work sessions with the dashboard as a support to read together the figures and discrepancies observed and to reflect on corrective actions jointly. In this way, the processes could be gradually modified, and the operational staff could be more involved in and responsible for the financial aspects of their structure.

Indeed, the observed involvement of the actors was not as great as expected at the beginning of the process. However, it is important to note that it is this involvement and the fact that the individuals could find their expectations fulfilled in the tool that allowed the project to succeed. To propose a participative construction approach using the framework of translation allows us to respond to the challenges of the SSE by combining the needs of control and the social and solidarity priorities of the operational staff.

NOTE.– It is necessary to combine two opposing conceptions:

– a response to the expectations of funders and modernization of the sector of activity through better management;

– strong human values.

The Apprentis d'Auteuil case study highlighted the importance of the organization's role. Indeed, it should make people aware that the management indicators mainly from accounting data allow decisions to be made and action to be taken to limit operating costs in order to generate additional resources that can be reused for new actions, in line with the social and solidarity objectives of the foundation. The communication of the organization and the taking into account of the needs of the stakeholders by customizing the tool have allowed us to develop a relevant, accepted and used tool.

4.3. A new way of managing?

The question of the balance between management and values predominates. The objective here is to question how organizations can maintain their activist values and identity without resembling a traditional company. In the two previous sections, we saw that it was necessary to be innovative in management control tools in order for them to be accepted and used despite the existing tensions with management control; in this section we see how an organization takes the opposite view of financial issues in order to reaffirm its values while supporting people in difficulty while respecting them is a priority. We will first see what management by values is. Then, we will study the case of the Protestant Sonnenhof Foundation. Finally, the role of innovation will be examined.

4.3.1. *Management by values*

The question of the balance between management and values is predominant here. This topic has been studied in particular by Château-Terrisse (2018). The author points out that the solution is to clarify the social and economic objectives and to translate them together into the contents of management tools so that they contribute to the collective construction of meaning. Indeed, "the adequacy of values, principles, rules and practices depends on the coherence of their application in all areas of management" (Parodi 2004). Nevertheless, there is still a risk:

> If the social and solidarity enterprise does not respect the guiding principles that define it, then it loses its legitimacy and jeopardizes its eventual survival. (Béji-Bécheur et al. 2018)

Godelier (2006) uses several examples of for-profit companies showing that the organization's culture and values are elements to be considered for them to be a support and not an obstacle. For example, the author cites the president of Shell, who insisted in 2000 on the importance of culture in change, or the merger of BNP and Paribas where the different values made the operation delicate. Corporate culture is defined by Godelier (1998) as "the set of principles, representations and values shared by the members of the same society and which organize their way of thinking and acting on their environment and themselves, to organize their relationships". Culture is seen as an element of performance (Sugita in Bazin and Sélim 1996). If culture is the result of a collective process of accumulation throughout history (Godelier 2006), values are the product of corporate culture (Le Goff 2003). They are moral or ethical.

In the social/solidarity-based economy, the values of solidarity, freedom, moral responsibility, equality and the primacy of human development are prevalent. Godelier (2006) indicates that management by values is synonymous with corporate culture and can be considered a management method. But values are general and not operational. This is why they are often broken down into behaviors that guide managers on a daily basis according to the situation. In order to carry out this project, Blanchard and O'Connor (1997) define the implementation of management by values in three stages:

– value clarification;

– communication of values;

– alignment of daily behaviors with values.

This is what we will cover in our case study. Indeed, to respond to the new challenges of the SSE and the necessity of favoring management, we observed how an organization establishes its values and culture of support for the other while profoundly transforming its management mode.

4.3.2. *The case of the Protestant Sonnenhof Foundation*

4.3.2.1. Context

The foundation is Protestant. It welcomes and accompanies people with intellectual disabilities and/or multiple disabilities, from childhood to the end of life, as well as dependent elderly people. It is located in Northern Alsace and has been in business for 143 years. As a true social and solidarity economy player, it manages about 20 establishments and employs more than 800 people. It has undergone profound modernization in recent years. In April 2014, a new general manager was appointed. As an ex-executive of private industry, she succeeded a general manager who had managed the foundation for nearly 20 years before being appointed president of the Council of the Union of Protestant Churches of Alsace and Lorraine. This change in leadership ushered in a new era for the foundation. The new executive director has breathed new life into the foundation of modernism, renewal and industry habits. Today, the foundation's mission can be summed up in this assertion: "All citizens, all innovators, all committed!"

Faced with an unstable context, shrinking budgets, the negotiation of multi-year contracts of objectives and means, a change in management as well as a desire to reaffirm the foundation's values in order to stabilize the situation, the board of directors and the management committee began work to redefine the foundation's core values.

This work of formalizing values had never been done within the foundation, one of the board of directors members expressed at first sight: "The values, we do not formalize them, they are in our hearts".

This transformation process was initiated to transform a social and solidarity organization into an economic, social and solidarity organization.

The goal is to get a collective of managers and foundation representatives to work together to deploy these values as best practices to be disseminated to all foundation members so that each manager can bring the foundation's values to life. It is this values working group that we study in this section.

4.3.2.2. Data collected

Data collection was initially accomplished through participation in the working group, summarized in Table 4.4.

Date	Type of meetings	Number of hours
19 March	Working group meeting	4
23 April	Working group meeting	4
31 May	Working group meeting	4
19 June	Working group meeting	4
28 August	Working group meeting	4
3 September	Working group meeting	2.5
10 September	Working group meeting	4
13 September	Presentation to the Management Committee	1.5
21 September	Presentation to the Extended Management Committee	3
12 November	Presentation to the Management Committee	3
Total	–	34

Table 4.4. Summary of participation in the working group

During these meetings, we took detailed notes and collected documents.

We complete this study with various interviews that are presented in Table 4.5. These interviews are semi-directive; they were recorded and then transcribed.

Function	Objectives	Number of hours
Executive Director	Understand the impetus for this values working group	2.0
Human Resources Director – member of the Management Committee	Obtain a vision of the repository conducted by the working group	0.5
Head of Management Control – member of the Extended Management Committee	Obtain a vision of the repository conducted by the working group	0.5
Facility Manager – member of the Steering Committee and Working Group		0.7
Total	–	3.7

Table 4.5. *Summary of interviewees*

4.3.2.3. *Results*

4.3.2.3.1. The work carried out by the working group

The work on the foundation's values began when the new executive director, who had recently arrived, asked the board of directors about the foundation's values and how they wanted them expressed. This institution had existed for a very long time and had grown over time, but its values and expression had never been formalized. The desire was therefore to rework the entire management system. This work was undertaken in 2017, with the arrival of a new human resources director. The new management system consists of four axes:

– the construction of a reference framework to provide a framework, a managerial posture, a role and responsibilities;

– organization with the setting up of management groups, a network operation;

– support with the implementation of an integration program, assistance in taking up a position, training;

– development through the organization of meetings, exchanges and thematic workshops.

The definition of the values was carried out before the development of these four axes. The values were defined by the management committee and the board of directors before our study. For the foundation, they represent the fundamental convictions according to which a specific mode of conduct or end state of existence would be personally or socially preferable to a contrary or opposite mode of conduct or end state of existence.

The four values are the following:

– Altruism: it is a benevolent and humble disposition toward others, whose objective is their fulfilment and development. It is therefore the ability to listen, to empathize, and to help/accomplish in order to achieve individual well-being (but without compromising the collective interest).

– Dignity: this is the feeling of the intrinsic value of a person or a thing, which commands respect for others. It is the principle that a person should never be treated as an object or a means, but as an intrinsic entity that deserves unconditional respect, regardless of age, gender, physical or mental health, social condition, religion or ethnic origin.

– Responsibility: it is an obligation for a person to be accountable for his or her actions because of the role, the responsibilities that he or she has to assume and to bear all the consequences of. It is therefore the capacity for the person to decide in full conscience, without referring beforehand to a superior authority, to be able to give the reasons/motivations of his or her acts, to be able to be evaluated on these last ones and to answer to consequences.

– Questioning: this is the regular questioning of one's state/practices in order to possibly modify them in order to improve. It is therefore the ability to correct one's action by a profound change (transformation), with means following existing rules, in order to reorganize and improve operations and results.

These values were presented to the expanded Management Committee at the end of 2017 with the announcement of the creation of a working group whose role was to express these values in terms of principles of action and then in terms of behavior. The idea was not to develop a guide for the perfect manager but to obtain benchmarks that could help when difficult situations arise.

Each value has been developed into a principle of action and then into the consequences of the main tasks that managers must perform (recruiting, leading, evaluating, training, securing, innovating, sanctioning, arbitrating, valuing, etc.).

This work was carried out over about 6 months, with several half-days of role-playing, brainstorming and discussions. A professor of practical theology took part in this work on the translation of values into induced behaviors. These interventions can be surprising initially, but they were an additional contribution to this work and were appreciated by all the participants. They helped to spiritualize the discussions, to give them a higher level and to give a deeper meaning to the values.

The framework was presented to the Management Committee and then to the extended Management Committee.

4.3.2.3.2. Participatory work

This work is participative since representatives of managers participated in the work group. This was a real asset for the appropriation of values by managers, but also for a better representation of the behaviors involved. For the director of human resources, the fact that this work was carried out by operational staff was a "condition" for the project to be carried out, and for the members of the working group, it was "obvious". In particular, it allowed for the harmonization of practices between the many establishments: if the values were the same, the behaviors could be radically different according to the experiences of each. The executive director testified that she did not want to "impose a standard values model". The behaviors induced by the values really need to come back into play; it is not a matter of changing the values, but of affirming them and harmonizing their meaning.

Opinions are very positive about the work carried out, provided that this reference framework lives on. The Human Resources Director explains that it should not be "a poster on a wall" but a real tool.

In addition to creating a reference framework, a manager who had been in charge of a school for many years expressed her need to step back from her daily work, to gain some perspective, "to nourish herself to nourish her teams". This work group responded to this expectation. She describes these moments as "happy" moments that allow her to escape her daily routine where everything goes too fast.

Although none of the interviewees have changed their management style since the creation of this reference framework, all of them express their satisfaction with the work carried out and the fact that they have formalized the values that have been with them since they joined the foundation. This will make it possible to transmit them. For the interviewees, it is not the frame of reference that will necessarily instigate a change in management, but rather that their paradigm will change as soon as they arrive at the foundation, compared to management in for-profit companies. One of the interviewees testifies that the values "transform the human in addition to the organization". Training and instilling these values will allow newcomers to be "less shaken by changes in context and new pressures, [and] the values will help them remember what is really important", according to one facility manager.

In addition, formalizing expected behaviors also makes it possible to harmonize practices between institutions where the expression of values may have been different, as the head of management control reminds us.

4.3.3. *Room for innovation*

The Protestant Sonnenhof Foundation has existed for 143 years and is steeped in values that have been defined for many years. The ideology of the institution remains the same. The revolution has been to formalize them, make them more specific, and involve the collective. The implementation of management by values is the study of the clarification of values, that is to say the first stage of the process of Blanchard and O'Connor (1997). The following steps of communication and alignment can be studied later.

As we have seen, this first stage is divided into two sub-phases:

– the clarification and choice of Protestant values in relation to the current issues that were conducted by the executive committee and the board of directors before our study;

– the translation of values into good practices that have been studied by the working group.

The changes that are taking place within the Protestant Sonnenhof Foundation are the translation of one of the major stages in the evolution of the organization that Rousseau calls the "factory of meaning" where the organization finds a dynamic balance between its economic development and the development of its project. These two aspects are no longer exclusive, but feed each other. Indeed, the management framework implemented by the foundation can be defined as a "tool for managing meaning" in order to "bring its social project and its production organization into line" (Rousseau 2007).

In response to an unstable environment due to the change in general management, a partial renewal of divisional management, the creation of support services and a context in crisis, the values of the foundation were at risk of being shaken. The executive director notes that "culture is not necessarily easy to manage", but it nevertheless reflects what the foundation is. Indeed, "there is always a caring hand that calms, that reassures the residents. In general [...] the employees accept a lot, because they feel they have a mission. It's dignified and noble"; "they have a culture of self-giving". Even if the foundation's priority is to provide the best possible support to the residents, it is necessary for the management to meet the sector's regulatory requirements and adapt to them. And this pressure is irremediably felt by the teams. The work instigated by the board of directors and the general management has made it possible to refocus on the values carried by the foundation. The management then sent a strong message to the employees. Indeed, the values were old, already carried by the employees, but transmitted informally. By setting up the working group, management recognizes its values, asserts them, encourages employees to do the same and places them in response to this environment, which wishes to stabilize itself, and to this restrictive context.

We, therefore, see a return to the identity of the structure by reaffirming the values. Godelier (2006, p. 40) points out that this phenomenon "leads to the burden of change being placed more heavily on individuals rather than on the organization, its choices or the means it takes on". Managers will need to reconcile the requirements of performance with the priorities of support and benevolence. Innovation seems to be an appropriate solution (Raedersdorf 2015). The general manager emphasizes that the objective is to put forward the principles of responsibility and subsidiarity by encouraging managers to listen. The idea is not to be a book of grievances, but to be benevolent toward all stakeholders.

Consistency is brought to the managers who embody these values. By defining what is considered positive behavior in the company, the reference framework accompanies the manager daily.

Château-Terrisse (2018) points out that the solution to the new challenges of the SSE is to clarify social and economic objectives and translate them into management content to contribute to meaning. At the Protestant Sonnenhof Foundation, the staff met and confirmed this demonstration insofar as establishing the values positively affected the managers.

To promote the implementation of this framework, the definition of values needed to be defined by those involved in the day-to-day management of the company. All the interviewees noted this point was a real success factor for this approach. Like the case study of the

Apprentis d'Auteuil Foundation (Raedersdorf 2018), where the author showed that the involvement of each person was a key factor of success, it is confirmed here that the participative approach is an essential element for the adhesion of managers. This method is an application of the answer given by Château-Terrisse (2018). Indeed, by encouraging the diversity of professional identities and the expression of each type of user, it is possible to build and use a management tool that is consistent with multiple purposes (financial and social). This was the case in this study, as a dozen individuals with different professions, qualifications and experience participated in the work group.

SUMMARY.–

We met another sector of activity where management control is also in tension: the social and solidarity economy.

This sector is characterized by its strong values, the search for financial equilibrium and the need to innovate. Through the study of different structures, we have observed the evolutionary nature of the management tools used to integrate voluntary and recent innovations. The objective of this common dynamic is to adapt the performance measurement tools to the sector's specific needs.

The more specific analysis of the management tool used within the eastern territory of the Apprentis d'Auteuil foundation has made it possible to discern that expressing creativity through the management tool promotes innovation in the organization in the services it offers.

We also noted the crucial role of the organization. It must make people aware that the management indicators, mainly derived from accounting data, allow decisions and actions to be taken to limit operating costs. This allows for the release of additional resources that can be reused for new actions in line with the social and solidarity objectives of the foundation.

The communication of the organization and taking into account the stakeholders' needs through the customization of the tool have allowed us to develop a relevant, accepted and used tool.

In the last study of this section, we also showed the very important role of the organization. The Protestant Sonnenhof Foundation has embarked on the creation of a management system. It has chosen to counteract financial pressures by prioritizing the foundation's values. This action has strengthened the management dynamics and cohesion between managers.

The different cases studied in the social and solidarity economy show that these organizations have been able to overcome the apparent conflict between the values of the social/solidarity-based economy and the needs of management. The influence of the organization, the gathering of collaborators around the same issue or the development of organizational innovation make it possible to respond to both the values and the control issues specific to these organizations. These innovative practices observed in the context of the tensions between management control and the values of the social economy are inspiring. It seems appropriate to ask ourselves about their use in for-profit organizations where we find tensions between management control and innovation.

Conclusion

The reader of this book does not come away from this with a methodology for managing innovation processes. Such an ambition would be utopian. Indeed, there is no perfect tool adapted to all or even adapted to certain types of organizations or innovations. Each organization tries to implement a combination of tools and practices adapted to the innovation developed, to the actors in place and to the needs of the moment, depending on the progress of the process.

However, the reader will better understand the ins and outs of managing innovation processes. We have highlighted that the problem of managing innovation processes is a real issue for organizations, which sometimes find themselves needing help when faced with the contradictions and interests of the various players. This book contributes to helping managers become aware of the reality of innovation process management in organizations.

In this conclusion, we propose to the reader a reflection on three main axes that emerge from this work for the management of innovation:

– the role of the organization;

– the balance between control and creativity;

– the integration of actors for innovative management.

Finally, we conclude our work by assessing the challenges for organizations today that go beyond the tensions between control and creativity and the significant contribution of management control tools.

C.1. The role of the organization

C.1.1. *The influence of the organization*

The organization will influence how employees will approach the existing tensions. This influence has already been suggested in the literature in the context of tensions between control and creativity. Indeed, it is by using management control tools that the organization will support or inhibit change (Touchais 2006). The results of Chapters 2 and 3 highlight the desire of organizations to use management control tools to manage the innovation processes. However, these qualitative studies show that the tools, although useful and necessary, are not necessarily adapted to the needs of the actors. For some of them, the tools are perceived as an additional administrative task, even though they recognize it as necessary. The tools are only sometimes perceived as a support to the project. In the for-profit organizations studied, the organization's influence is strong, and it provides the actors with the answer to the question: "How can the innovation process be managed?" Employees in charge of innovation must use these tools, but very often, they need to be adapted, and informal practices or hidden tools are put in place to carry out parallel monitoring.

Chapter 4, through the study of the social and solidarity economy sector, has allowed us to go further into the role of organizations in the face of tensions. Indeed, by drawing on the theory of attention (Ocasio 1997), which relates the behavior of companies in the channeling and distribution of attention to the choices made by decision-makers, it makes it possible to reconcile democratic functioning and economic success (Gand 2015) and to deal with the natural tensions between management control and operational objectives, which are more social and solidarity based, in particular by recalling the objectives and interests of the project. The influence of the organization and its role in the allocation and the distribution of the attention of the actors allowed for the successful implementation of a management control tool in an environment of tension that has allowed, as we see in the last part, to stabilize the conflicts between the strong values and the financial pressures imposed on the employees. Indeed, the organization creates an environment conducive to the expression of values and provides the means to achieve this without excluding the need for control. In social and solidarity economy organizations, organizations have gone beyond "how to manage" to provide actors with answers to the question "Why manage?" These meaningful answers allow actors creative freedom in their day-to-day management of the way they manage. In their work, Szostak et al. (2013) emphasize the role of these spaces of freedom, which allow the implementation of adapted management tools.

These essential roles of the organization in managing conflicts lead us to reconsider the place of the organization in managing tensions between control and creativity. The organization has a role to play in creating an environment conducive to innovation and expressing its employees' creativity. It has the responsibility to find the right level of control to leave the door open for the expression of creativity, allowing for innovation. If the pressure is too great, it risks annihilating all creativity or encouraging a phenomenon of job strain (Karasek and Robert 1979) wherein employees are disenchanted. The high level of tension and the high psychological demands leave little space for employees. The role of the organization is, therefore, essential.

C.1.2. *Organization as a source of creativity*

Given its influence, the organization must use the levers at its disposal to set the tone and encourage creativity implementing appropriate management control tools. To put in place tools that encourage innovation, the concept of organizational learning and theories of actions will help us. It proposes to distinguish between the theory in use and the espoused theory as defined by Argyris and Schön (2002). The theory in use corresponds to the strategies of effective actions. In contrast, the espoused theory corresponds to the values, beliefs and attitudes that are the basis of the production of the discourse. In Chapter 2, we highlighted the representation of managing innovation processes using the analogy of an iceberg. The emerging part of this iceberg comprises the existing, used and accepted formal management control tools. In contrast, the submerged part represents the informal practices that are widely used. The espoused theory that gives rise to discourse production mainly uses formal and conventional tools. The theory of use represents the submerged part of the iceberg, where we find informal practices that are widely used but not communicated to the outside world. To encourage creativity and make the organization progress, implementing a systematic questioning logic is recommended. A direct link has been established between implementing controls and promoting organizational learning (Argyris 1993; Bouquin 2008). Organizational learning is seen as a collective phenomenon that will modify the management of situations (Koenig 2006). The implementation of management control tools can therefore facilitate understanding a phenomenon and encourage questioning, which can give rise to new ideas and, thus, the development of innovations.

C.2. The balance between control and creativity

In the previous section, we discussed the organization's role in finding a balance between management control and creativity. However, it may sometimes be a matter of the organization accepting the existence of an imbalance.

C.2.1. *The search for balance to find a consensus between the actors*

Chapter 3 highlighted that organizations want to put management control tools in place to drive the tools in order to manage the innovation process. We therefore place ourselves in the current literature in favor of management tools. However, the existing tools still need to be optimal and only suit some businesses. Our data analysis shows a desire for consensus between the different actors and therefore between the different professions. This consensus is desired in the decision-making process of the organizations surveyed and is systematic at Fluido. This standardization of opinions is sought because of the uncertain nature of the innovation process and allows for greater assurance and confidence in the decision-making process. Consent is obtained through negotiation, or even political games, and this often informal interactivity allows the impact of management control tools to be nuanced. The interactivity of the tools encourages innovation (Simons 1995b) and according to Touchais (2006):

– They can be a source of change, as highlighted in Chapter 4. The innovation and interactivity of the management control tools studied in the social economy have made it possible to encourage innovation in the services offered.

– They can show a need, in the social and solidarity-based economy, for a new way of working, as we saw in Chapter 4 with the Protestant Sonnenhof Foundation case study. In the social economy, implementing a management by values has helped to rebalance tensions. The implementation of a new frame of reference, through a working group where interactivity was the basis, conveyed a strong message from the management, which recalled its priorities.

– They can build and structure the change, which we have highlighted in the case study of the Apprentis d'Auteuil Foundation. Because of the interactivity, the new management control tool has found its place. In for-profit organizations, the first three chapters have shown that management tools are desired to drive the changes necessary to develop an innovation.

Interactivity is therefore essential to find a balance between the tensions of management control and the values of the SSE or between management control and creativity. Moreover, this interactivity also resolves tensions between different practices and professions. Interactivity also takes on its whole meaning when formal and informal practices are mixed, as recommended by Ouchi (1979). As observed in both for-profit and not-for-profit contexts, these two types of control are complementary (Guibert and Dupuy 1997) and allow actors to ensure a complete management of the innovation process. We found this combination of practices in the cases studied in this book. The study of these cases has led us to place formal tools in the role of a safeguard according to the classification proposed by Lambert and Sponem (2009).

C.2.2. *Acceptance of an imbalance*

However, if the search for a balance is understandable, it seems dangerous to us to reach it. Indeed, the search for the ideal tool pushes organizations to reflect constantly and therefore to constantly question themselves. An imbalance favors organizational creativity and therefore innovation. Burlaud (2000) suggests the use of new control and measurement tools and it seems interesting to us to be in perpetual search of an adapted management tool. An imbalance can then be accepted and encourage creativity and innovation.

This imbalance can be different according to the stages of the process and thus be more marked at the beginning of the project than at the end. It also makes it possible to have tools that are constantly evolving and adapting to needs. The tools then evolve according to the projects, the actors and the project's progress. When the tools adapt to the needs, the actors use them and they are then perceived as a real support and no longer as a required administrative burden. We have demonstrated this in the case study of the Apprentis d'Auteuil Foundation. Thus, if the organization can influence the individuals, the tools also influence the organization and can therefore foster innovation. In the case of the Apprentis d'Auteuil Foundation, we have seen that the imbalance between values and control was accepted and asserted and that it became a vector of communication between the organization's leaders and employees. The top managers then represent the mediators.

C.3. Integrating actors with different needs and expectations to innovate within the tools and practices put in place

We have talked about organizational learning, but "it is not because a control system produces, disseminates or mobilizes knowledge that it will generate learning. It is necessary that this knowledge be 'accepted' by the decision-maker" (Batac and Carassus 2012, p. 69). The involvement of the actors is essential to initiate questioning. Integrating all stakeholders in the management process has emerged as a fundamental element of our work. Our work is in line with Szostak et al. (2018) because it is not so much the tool that needs to be different or adapted, but rather the appropriation of the tool that is primordial, and the integration of all stakeholders is therefore essential. For these authors, the question to be asked is not how to preserve the values of the SSE but "thanks to whom" (Szostak et al. 2018, p. 129) these values are preserved.

The theory of translation (Latour and Woolgar 1979; Callon 1981, 1986; Latour 1987; Dreveton and Rocher 2010) proposes to take into account the interests of the different stakeholders and thus to encourage mobilization and synergy in the long term around the project. The case of Apprentis d'Auteuil shows that the involvement of stakeholders throughout the innovation is a key success factor. In the case of the Sonnenhof Protestant Foundation, we studied implementing a management by values framework, by managers and for managers. Once again, the participation of the different actors made it possible to convey a message and a way of doing things to the whole organization. The exploratory study of innovation processes conducted in Chapter 2 shows that the rejection of tools imposed by management represents an administrative burden. The actors have therefore set up unofficial tools in parallel. We believe that it is essential to include all the actors in the reflection on an adapted tool so that it is relevant and accepted. It is also a question of the actors expressing their creativity through the tool. It is in the organization's interest to leave the door open to innovation management. This contributes to creating an environment conducive to the expression and development of innovation. The difficulty of motivating and integrating the players in a management project has been noted throughout this book. The organization must make a significant effort to obtain the support of the collaborators.

Figure C.1 summarizes the various elements of the organizational context of the social and solidarity economy that can be a source of inspiration for the management of the innovation processes. We find three blocks: the organization, the manager and the actors in the field. In this figure, we find a strong involvement of the organization, whose role is to define its strategy and provide answers to the question: "Why drive innovation?"

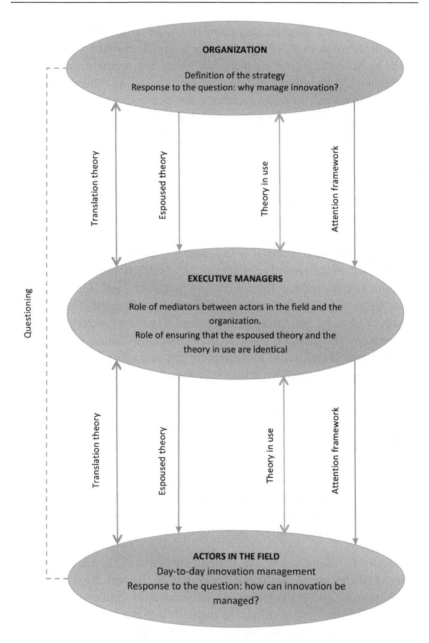

Figure C.1. *Elements of the organizational context to be taken into account for the management of innovation processes*

By using the attention framework, it will be able to generate interest and motivation. Their role is that of a mediator between the other two entities. Senior managers understand the needs and expectations of both the organization and the field. They use the framework of attention to communicate with the field and use translation theory to go back and forth between the field and the organization.

If the actors in the field answer the question "How do we drive innovation?" the executives make sure that the espoused theory and the theory in use are aligned around the same objectives.

Even if we go farther than Getz and Carney (2016), we come close. These authors highlight through an ethnographic study that it is possible to opt for radically different organizational forms that perform well and have a strong capacity for innovation. The authors show that the companies studied consider all employees to be intrinsically equal. By giving them the freedom to act, their actions will become more meaningful, and their motivation will increase. Creativity is then reinforced (Bollinger and Neukam forthcoming).

This search for meaning is particularly emblematic of the social and solidarity-based economy. The employees need this sense of purpose. The motto of the Protestant Sonnenhof Foundation is "Every life is a light". The organization sends the message that it is necessary to turn the paradigm around and no longer see disability as a burden, but as an asset in society. This different communication shows the trust and freedom that is given to people with a disability and to the voluntary initiatives of the employees.

While our message is less extreme than Getz and Carney (2016), we find it interesting to draw on them and consider the ways of the social and solidarity economy as a benchmark for for-profit organizations. The challenge is to go beyond the confrontation we find between control and creativity in order to make a managerial leap. The objective is to reach an accepted imbalance, allowing for the constant renewal of practices and thus promoting a double-loop learning process. Béji-Bécheur and Codello-Guijarro (2015) point out that allowing the expression of tensions and fostering a discourse around hybridity can be a source of performance.

C.4. What are the challenges in 2023?

The work presented in this book was conducted from 2015 to 2019. Always with the need to innovate in order to survive in a long-term perspective, these works remain of a burning topicality to help the organizations to manage their innovation process. However, more than simply taking into account the tension between control and creativity is required. As we saw in Chapter 4, we are questioning the meaning of innovation.

This question of meaning is becoming essential in the face of the new societal and environmental challenges that companies in 2023 must face. The second part of the sixth assessment report of the Intergovernmental Panel on Climate Change (IPCC) published on 28 February 2022 highlights that half of the world's population is already living in a high vulnerability to climate change. By 2050, 1 billion people living in coastal regions will be directly threatened by rising sea levels or marine submersion (Intergovernmental Panel on Climate Change 2022).

Climate change also poses unquestionable risks to businesses' environmental and social ecosystems. Our economy, highly dependent on natural resources, agriculture, development activities, energy and water, is therefore sensitive to the associated risks of drought. While these data exist and have been put forward by scientists for many years, we are now at a point where these issues can no longer be ignored.

Society expects companies to be committed and this is directly reflected in the motivation of employees (Bollinger and Neukam forthcoming). Therefore, companies are under pressure to make a real commitment and develop intelligent and creative innovations that incorporate a responsible approach (Neukam and Bollinger 2022). A company can no longer develop innovative products or services for society. According to the Edelman Trust Barometer, the population continuously loses trust in companies, and 56% of the participants believe that capitalism harms society. It seems that technological performance and development are disconnected from the needs and demands of society (Retolaza et al. 2020). Therefore, more than innovation is needed to create a competitive advantage. Companies must rehumanize their business model at all levels and with all stakeholders (Hamel 2020).

Therefore, the next generation of successful companies will innovate by responding simultaneously to social and environmental challenges. But this raises the question of the role of management control mechanisms. If, in this book, we have dealt with the tensions between control and creativity, we will add a third dimension of societal commitments. Once again, we find divergent views between these three dimensions. Commitment, innovation and financial performance must be brought together around a raison d'être and not be considered separate elements that coexist independently, creating tensions between them (Bollinger and Neukam 2021).

References

Abernethy, M.A. and Brownell, P. (1997). Management control systems in research and development organizations: The role of accounting, behavior and personnel controls. *Accounting, Organizations and Society*, 22(3), 233–248.

Abrahamson, E. and Rosenkopf, L. (1993). Institutional and competitive bandwagons: Using mathematical modeling as a tool to explore innovation diffusion. *Academy of Management Review*, 18(3), 487–517.

Acquier, A., Daudigeos, T., Valiorgue, B. (2011). Corporate social responsibility as an organizational and managerial challenge: The forgotten legacy of the Corporate Social Responsiveness movement. *Management*, 14(4), 222–250.

Adams, R., Bessant, J., Phelps, R. (2006). Innovation management measurement: A review. *International Journal of Management Reviews*, 8, 21–47.

Adler, P.S. and Chen, C.X. (2011). Combining creativity and control: Understanding individual motivation in large-scale collaborative creativity. *Accounting, Organizations & Society*, 36(2), 63–85.

Agro, L., Cornet, A., Pichault, F. (1996). Système d'information : quelle implication pour les utilisateurs ? *Revue française de gestion*, 110, 46–55.

Ahrens, T. and Chapman, C.S. (2004). Accounting for flexibility and efficiency: A field study of management control systems in a restaurant chain. *Contemporary Accounting Research*, 21(2), 271–301.

Aktouf, O., Boiral, O., Mehran, E., Saives, A. (2006). *Management entre tradition et renouvellement*, 4th edition. Gaëtan Morin, Boucherville.

Aldrich, H. and Fiol, C.M. (1994). Fools rush in? The institutional context of industry creation. *Academy of Management Review*, 19(4), 645–670.

Alter, N. (1998). Organisation et innovation, une rencontre conflictuelle. *Sciences Humaines*, 20(special edition), 185–192.

Altshuller, G., Shulyak, L., Rodman, S. (1997). *40 Principles: TRIZ Keys to Technical Innovation*. Technical Innovation Centre, Worcester.

Amabile, T.M. (1998). How to kill creativity? *Harvard Business Review*, 76(5), 76–87.

Amabile, T.M., Conti, R., Coon, H., Lazenby, J., Herron, M. (1996). Assessing the work environment for creativity. *Academy of Management Journal*, 39(5), 1154–1184.

Anderson, N., Potočnik, K., Zhou, J. (2014). Innovation and creativity in organizations: A state-of-the-science review, prospective commentary, and guiding framework. *Journal of Management*, 40(5), 1297–1333.

André, K. (2015). Une évaluation hybride des entreprises sociales. *Revue française de gestion*, 247(2), 71–83.

Arena, L. and Solle, G. (2012). Apprentissage organisationnel et contrôle de gestion : une lecture possible de l'ABC/ABM ? *Comptabilité contrôle audit*, 14(3), 67–85.

Argyris, C. (1993). *Knowledge for Action: A Guide to Overcoming Barriers to Organizational Change*. Jossey-Bass Inc, San Francisco [Online]. Available at: http://eric.ed.gov/?id=ED357268.

Argyris, C. and Schön, D.A. (2002). *Apprentissage organisationnel : théorie, méthode, pratique*. De Boeck, Louvain-la-Neuve.

Balachandra, R. and Friar, J. (1997) Factors for success in R&D projects and new product innovation: A contextual framework. *IEEE Transactions on Engineering Management*, 44, 276–287.

Banerjee, A.V. (1992). A simple model of herd behavior. *The Quaterly Journal of Economics*, 107(3), 797–817.

Barreto, I. and Baden-Fuller, C. (2006). To conform or to perform? Mimetic behaviour, legitimacy-based groups and performance consequences. *Journal of Management Studies*, 43(7), 1559–1581.

Barreyre, P.Y. (1980). Typologie des innovations. *Revue française de gestion*, 27, 9–15.

Batac, J. and Carassus, D. (2012). Les interactions contrôle-apprentissage organisationnel dans le cas d'une municipalité : une étude comparative avec Kloot (1997). *Comptabilité contrôle audit*, 14(3), 87–111.

Battilana, J. (2010). Building sustainable hybrid organizations: The case of commercial microfinance organizations. *The Academy of Management Journal*, 53(6), 1419–1440.

Baudonnière, P.-M. (1998). *Le mimétisme et l'imitation*. Flammarion, Paris.

Bayle, E. and Dupuis, J.C. (2012). *Management des entreprises de l'économie sociale et solidaire*. De Boeck, Louvain-la-Neuve [Online]. Available at: https://www.cairn.info/management-des-entreprises-de-l-economie-sociale-e-9782804170912.htm.

Bazin, L. and Sélim, M. (1996). Un symptôme unique : l'entreprise. *Journal des anthropologues*, 66–67, 11–18.

Bedford, D.S., Malmi, T., Sandelin, M. (2016). Management control effectiveness and strategy: An empirical analysis of packages and systems. *Accounting, Organizations and Society*, 51, 12–28.

Béji-Bécheur, A. and Codello-Guijarro, P. (2015). L'hybridité de l'entreprise sociale et solidaire : facteur de performance ? *Revue française de gestion*, 247(2), 69–70.

Béji-Bécheur, A., Diaz Pedregal, V., Ozcaglar-Toulouse, N. (2008). Fair trade – Just how "fair" are the exchanges? *Journal of Macromarketing*, 28(1), 44–52.

Béji-Bécheur, A., Codello, P., Château-Terrisse, P. (2018). Avantpropos de GESS – Gestion des entreprises sociales et solidaires. In *GESS : Gestion des entreprises sociales et solidaires*. EMS, Caen.

Ben Mahmoud-Jouini, S. and Charue-Duboc, F. (2014). Le déploiement d'innovations inter-filiales au sein d'une multinationale. *Management international*, 18, 42–58.

Benner, M.J. and Tushman, M.L. (2003). Exploitation, exploration, and process management: The productivity dilemma revisited. *Academy of Management Review*, 28(2), 238–256.

Berland, N. and Persiaux, F. (2008). Le contrôle des projets d'innovation de haute technologie. *Comptabilité contrôle audit*, 14(2), 75–106.

Berland, N., Chevalier-Kuszla, C., Sponem, S. (2008). On ne gère bien que ce que l'on mesure. In *Petit bréviaire des idées reçues en management*, Critique et Management (CriM), Pezet, A., Sponem, S. (eds). La Découverte, Paris [Online]. Available at: https://www.cairn.info/petit-breviaire-des-idees-recues-en-management-9782707160140-page-157.htm.

Berry, M. (1983). Une technologie invisible – L'impact des instruments de gestion sur l'évolution des systèmes humains. *Cahier du laboratoire*, CRG-1133.

Bezes, P. and Demazière, D. (2011). Introduction de "New Public Management et professions dans l'État : au-delà des oppositions, quelles recompositions ? *Sociologie du travail*, 53(3), 293–305.

Bidet, É. (2003). L'insoutenable grand écart de l'économie sociale Isomorphisme institutionnel et économie solidaire. *Revue du MAUSS*, 21(1), 162–178.

Bikhchandani, S., Hirshleifer, D., Welch, I. (1992). A theory of fads, fashion, custom, and cultural change as informational cascades. *The Journal of Political Economy*, 100(5), 992–1026.

Blanchard, K. and O'Connor, M. (1997). *Managing by Values. How to Put Your Values into Action for Extraordinary Results*. Berrett-Koehler, San Francisco.

Boitier, M. and Rivière, A. (2011). Changement et institutionnalisation des systèmes de contrôle de gestion : proposition d'un cadre d'analyse institutionnel enrichi. *Management & avenir*, 5(45), 80–100.

Bollinger, S. (2020). La place des outils de contrôle de gestion dans le pilotage des processus d'innovation. *ACCRA*, 7(1), 63–83.

Bollinger, S. and Burger-Helmchen, T. (2021). Du contrôle de l'innovation à la créativité : vers un cadre intégrateur. *Revue d'économie industrielle*, 174, 223–247.

Bollinger, S. and Neukam, M. (2021). Innovation and altruism: A new paradigm defining the survival of corporations? In *Integrated Science*, Rezaei, N. (ed.). Springer International Publishing, Cham [Online]. Available at: https://link.springer.com/10.1007/978-3-030-65273-9_21.

Bollinger, S. and Martinez-Diaz, C. (2022). Pilotage des processus d'innovation entre contrôle et créativité : étude exploratoire des outils et pratiques. *Marchés et organisations*, 45(3), 111–146.

Bollinger, S. and Neukam, M. (forthcoming). Les valeurs de l'organisation, moteur de la créativité. In *Gouvernance des innovations sociales*. Epure/Presses Universitaires de Reims.

Bonner, J.M. (2005). The influence of formal controls on customer interactivity in new product development. *Industrial Marketing Management*, 34(1), 63–69.

Bouchard, V. and Bos, C. (2006). Dispositifs intrapreneuriaux et créativité organisationnelle. *Revue française de gestion*, 2(161), 95–109.

Bouquin, H. (1994). *Les fondements du contrôle de gestion*. Presses Universitaires de France, Paris.

Bouquin, H. (2008). *Le contrôle de gestion*. Presses Universitaires de France, Paris.

Bouquin, H. and Fiol, M. (2007). Le contrôle de gestion : repères perdus, espace à retrouver. In *28ᵉ congrès de l'Association Francophone de Comptabilité*. Poitiers.

Bourguignon, A. (1995). La performance, essais de définition. *Revue française de comptabilité*, 26, 61–66.

Boussard, V. (2008). *Sociologie de la gestion. Les faiseurs de performance*. Belin [Online]. Available at: http://journals.openedition.org/lectures/633.

Bovais, H. (2014). Le pluralisme intégré, pierre angulaire des organisations hybrides. *Revue française de gestion*, 240(3), 97–114.

Broadbent, J. and Laughlin, R. (2009). Performance management systems: A conceptual model. *Management Accounting Research*, 20, 283–295.

Burger-Helmchen, T. and Raedersdorf, S. (2018). *Pro en Management*. Vuibert, Paris.

Burlaud, A. (2000). Contrôle et gestion. In *Encyclopédie de comptabilité, contrôle de gestion et audit*, Colasse, B. (ed.). Economica, France.

Callon, M. (1981). Struggles and negotiations to define what is problematic and what is not. In *The Social Process of Scientific Investigation*, Knorr, K.D., Krohn, R., Whitley, R. (eds). Springer, Dordrecht [Online]. Available at: https://doi.org/10.1007/978-94-009-9109-5_8.

Callon, M. (1986). Some elements of a sociology of translation: Domestication of the scallops and the fishermen of St Brieuc Bay. *The Sociological Review*, 32(1), 196–233.

Callon, M. and Latour, B. (2006). Le grand Léviathan s'apprivoise-t-il ? In *Sociologie de la traduction*, Akrich, M., Callon, M., Latour, B. (eds). Presses des Mines, Paris [Online]. Available at: http://books. openedition.org/pressesmines/1190.

Capron, M. (2012). Finalité(s) et performance(s) des entreprises de l'E.S.S. In *Management des entreprises de l'économie sociale et solidaire*, Bayle, E. and Dupuis, J.C. (eds). De Boeck, Louvain-la-Neuve [Online]. Available at: https://www.lgdj.fr/management-des-entreprises-de-l-economie-sociale-et-solidaire-9782804170912.html.

Cardinal, L.B., Sitkin, S.B., Long, C.P. (2004). Balancing and rebalancing in the creation and evolution of organizational control. *Organization Science*, 15(4), 411–431.

Chanal, V. and Mothe, C. (2005). Comment concilier innovation d'exploitation et innovation d'exploration : une étude de cas dans le secteur automobile. *Revue française de gestion*, 31(154), 173–191.

Chang, L. and Birckett, B. (2004). Managing intellectual capital in a professional service firm: Exploring the creativity-productivity paradox. *Management Accounting Research*, 15(1), 7–31.

Chanlat, J.-F. (1998). *Sciences sociales et management : plaidoyer pour une anthropologie générale*. Presses Université Laval, Quebec.

Château-Terrisse, P. (2015). Les mécanismes de coordination de pactes d'actionnaires dans la finance solidaire. *Revue française de gestion*, 246(1), 111–126.

Château-Terrisse, P. (2018). Réconcilier les organisations de l'ESS avec les outils de gestion. In *GESS : Gestion des entreprises sociales et solidaires*. EMS, Caen.

Chemin, C. and Gilbert, P. (2010). L'évaluation de la performance, analyseur de la gouvernance associative. *Politiques et management public*, 15, 55–78.

Chenhal, R.H. (2003). Management control systems design within its organizational context: Findings from contingency-based research and directions for the future. *Accounting Organizations and Society*, 28, 127–168.

Chesbrough, H.W. (2006). *Open Innovation: The New Imperative for Creating and Profiting from Technology*. Harvard Business School Press, Boston.

Chiapello, E. (1990). Contrôleurs de gestion, comment concevez-vous votre fonction ? *Échanges*, 92, 7–11.

Chiapello, E. (1997). Les organisations et le travail artistiques sont-ils contrôlables ? *Réseaux*, 15(86), 77–113.

Chiapello, E. (1998). *Artistes versus managers – Le management culturel face à la critique artiste*. Métailié, Paris.

Chiva-Gomez, R., Alegre-Vidal, J., Lapiedra-Alcami, R. (2004). A model of product design management in the Spanish ceramic sector. *European Journal of Innovation Management*, 7(2), 150–161.

Christensen, C.M. (1997). *The Innovator's Dilemma: When New Technologies Cause Great Firms to Fail*. Harvard Business School Press, Boston.

Christensen, C.M., Kaufman, S.P., Shih, W.C. (2008). Innovation killers: How financial tools destroy your capacity to do new things. *Harvard Business Review* [Online]. Available at: https://hbr. org/2008/01/innovation-killers-how-financial-tools-destroy-your-capacity-to-do-new-things.

Codello-Guijarro, P. and Béji-Bécheur, A. (2015). Les entreprises sociales et solidaires à l'épreuve des outils de gestion. *Revue française de gestion*, 246(1), 103–109.

Cohendet, P. (1997). Apprentissage organisationnel et cohérence : l'importance économique du réseau. In *Les limites de la rationalité. Rationalité, éthique et cognition*, volume 2, Reynaud, B. (ed.). La Découverte, Paris.

Cohendet, P. and Simon, L. (2015). Introduction to the special issue on creativity in innovation. *Technology Innovation Management Review*, 5(7), 5–13.

Cohendet, P., Bas, C.L., Simon, L., Szostak, B. (2013). La gestion de la créativité. *Gestion*, 38(3), 5–5.

Coombs, R., Saviotti, P., Walsh, V. (1987). *Economics and Technological Change*. Macmillan, London.

Cooper, R.G. (1979a). Identifying industrial new product success: Project NewProd. *Industrial Marketing Management*, 8, 124–135.

Cooper, R.G. (1979b). The dimensions of industrial new product success and failure. *Journal of Marketing*, 43, 93–103.

Cooper, R.G. (2001). *Winning at New Products: Accelerating the Process from Idea to Launch*, 3rd edition. Basic Books, New York.

Cooper, R.G. and Kleinschmidt, E.J. (1987). New products: What separates winners from losers? *Journal of Product Innovation Management*, 4(3), 169–184.

Cooper, R.G. and Kleinschmidt, E.J. (1995). Benchmarking the firm's critical success factors in new product development. *Journal of Product Innovation Management*, 12(5), 374–391.

Covaleski, M., Dirsmith, M., Samuel, S. (1996). Managerial accounting research: The contributions of organizational and sociological theories. *Journal of Management Accounting Research*, 8, 1–35.

CRESS (2013). Elles et ils innovent. Chambre régionale de l'économie sociale et solidaire d'Alsace [Online]. Available at: https://www.calameo.com/books/004906765f95de4330f0a.

Damanpour, F. (1991). Organizational innovation: A meta-analysis of effects of determinants and moderators. *Academy of Management Journal*, 34(3), 555–590.

Dangereux, K., Chapellier, P., Villesèque-Dubus, F. (2017a). Nature et rôle des outils de contrôle de gestion dans les PME innovantes. In *L'innovation managériale : les multiples voies d'une spirale vertueuse*, Mignon, S., Chapellier, P., Mazars-Chapelon, A., Villesèque-Dubus, F. (eds). EMS, Caen.

Dangereux, K., Chapellier, P., Villesèque-Dubus, F. (2017b). Chapitre 7. Nature et rôle des outils de contrôle de gestion dans les PME innovantes. In *L'innovation managériale : les multiples voies d'une spirale vertueuse*, Mignon, S., Chapellier, P., Mazars-Chapelon, A., Villesèque-Dubus, F. (eds). EMS, Caen [Online]. Available at: https://doi.org/10.3917/ems.migno.2017.01.0167.

Davila, T. (2000). An empirical study on the drivers of management control systems' design in new product development. *Accounting, Organizations and Society*, 25(4/5), 383–409.

Davila, T. (2010). Thoughts on the structure of management systems to encourage creativity and innovation. In *Performance Measurement and Managerial Control: Innovative Concepts and Practices*. Epstein, R., Manzoni, J.-F., Davila, T. (eds). Emerald Group, Plymouth.

Davila, A., Foster, G., Li, M. (2009). Reasons for management control systems adoption: Insights from product development systems choice by early-stage entrepreneurial companies. *Accounting, Organizations and Society*, 34, 322–347.

De Brentani, U. (1991). Success factors in developing new business services. *European Journal of Marketing*, 25, 33–60.

Demoustier, D. (2002). Une lecture française : l'analyse proposée par Claude Vienney est-elle encore pertinente aujourd'hui ? In *Coopération et économie sociale au "second" XXe siècle : Claude Vienney (1929–2001)*, Chomel, A. (ed.). L'Harmattan, Paris.

Demoustier, D. and Malo, M.C. (2012). L'économie sociale et solidaire : une économie relationnelle ? Questions d'identité et de stratégie ! In *Management des entreprises de l'économie sociale et solidaire*, Bayle, E. and Dupuis, J.C. (eds). De Boeck, Louvain-la-Neuve.

Dent, J. (1990). Strategy, organization and control: Some possibilities for accounting research. *Accounting, Organizations and Society*, 15(1–2), 3–25.

Desrosières, A. (2008). *L'argument statistique*. Presses des Mines, Paris.

Di Benedetto, C.A. (1996). Identifying the key success factors in new product launch. *Journal of Product Innovation Management*, 16, 530–544.

Dillard, J., Rigsby, J., Goodman, C. (2004). The making and remaking of organization context: Duality and the institutionalization process. *Accounting, Auditing and Accountability Journal*, 17(4), 506–542.

DiMaggio, P. and Powell, W. (1983). The iron cage revisited: Institutionalized isomorphism and collective rationality in organizational fields. *American Sociological Review*, 48(2), 147–160.

Ditillo, A. (2004). Dealing with uncertainty in knowledge-intensive firms: The role of management control systems as knowledge integration mechanisms. *Accounting, Organizations and Society*, 29(3/4), 401–421.

Dreveton, B. and Rocher, S. (2010). "Lost in translation", étude de la construction d'un outil de gestion dans une région française. *Comptabilité contrôle audit*, 16(1), 83–100.

Drucker, P.F. (1985). *Innovation and Entrepreneurship: Practice and Principles*. Harper Business, New York.

Drucker, P.F. (2002). The discipline of innovation. *Harvard Business Review*, 1 August [Online]. Available at: https://hbr.org/2002/08/the-discipline-of-innovation.

Dubouloz, S. (2014). Innovation organisationnelle et pratiques de mobilisation des RH. *Revue française de gestion*, 1(238), 59–85.

Dumoulin, R. and Simon, É. (2005). Stratégie de rupture et PME : la réplication impossible. *Revue française de gestion*, 155(2), 75–95.

Durand, T. (1992). Dual technological trees: Assessing the intensity and strategic significance of technological change. *Research Policy*, 21(4), 361–380.

Dutton, J., Ashford, S.J., O'Neill, R.M., Lawrence, K.A. (2001). Moves that matter: Issue selling and organizational change. *Academy of Management Journal*, 44, 716–736.

Enjolras, B. (1998). Crise de l'État-providence, lien social et associations : éléments pour une socio-économie critique. *La Revue du MAUSS*, 11, 233–234.

Ernst, H. (2002). Success factors of new product development: A review of the empirical literature. *International Journal of Management Reviews*, 4, 1–40.

Fernez-Walch, S. and Romon, F. (2013). *Management de l'innovation de la stratégie aux projets*. Vuibert, Paris.

Ferreira, A. and Otley, D. (2009). The design and use of performance management systems: An extended framework for analysis. *Management Accounting Research*, 20(4), 263–282.

Forbes, D.P. (1998). Measuring the unmeasurable: Empirical studies of nonprofit organization effectiveness from 1977 to 1997. *Nonprofit and Voluntary Sector Quarterly*, 27(2), 183–202.

Freeman, C. and Pérez, C. (1988). Structural crises of adjustment, business cycles and investment behavior. In *Technical Change and Economic Theory*, Dosi, G., Freeman, C., Nelson, R., Silverberg, G., Soete, L. (eds). Pinter, London.

Freeman, C. and Soete, L. (1997). *The Economics of Industrial Innovation*, 3rd edition. Psychology Press, Cambridge.

Frigo, M.L. and Litman, J. (2007). *Driven: Business Strategy, Human Actions, and the Creation of Wealth*. Strategy & Execution, Chicago.

Galaskiewicz, J. and Wasserman, S. (1989). Mimetic processes within an interorganizational field: An empirical test. *Administrative Science Quarterly*, 34(3), 454–479.

Gand, S. (2015). Gouvernance démocratique et circulation des savoirs – Quels dispositifs de gestion? *Revue française de gestion*, 41(246), 127–142.

Gantt, H.L. (1913). *Work, Wages, and Profits*. Kessinger Publishing, LLC, Whitefish.

Getz, I. and Carney, B. (2016). *Liberté & cie : quand la liberté des salariés fait le succès des entreprises*. Flammarion, Paris.

Gilbert, P. (1998). *L'instrumentation de gestion. La technologie de gestion, science humaine ?* Economica, Paris.

Gilson, L.L., Mathieu, J.E., Shalley, C.E., Ruddy, T.M. (2005). Creativity and standardization: Complementary or conflicting drivers of team effectiveness? *Academy of Management Journal*, 48(3), 521–531.

Giordano, Y. (2003). *Conduire un projet de recherche : une perspective qualitative*. EMS, Caen.

Girard, R. (1972). *La violence et le sacré*. Hachette, Paris.

Godelier, M. (1998). La culture est-elle naturelle? In *La culture est-elle naturelle ? Histoire, épistémologie et applications récentes du concept de culture*, Ducros, A., Ducros, J., Joulian, F. (eds). Errance, Paris.

Godelier, E. (2006). *La culture d'entreprise*. La Découverte, Paris.

Gomez, P.Y. (1996). *Le gouvernement de l'entreprise*. Interéditions, Paris.

Griffin, A. (1997). PDMA research on new product development practices: Updating trends and benchmarking best practices. *Journal of Product Innovation Management*, 14, 429–458.

Grimes, M. (2010). Strategic sensemaking within funding relationships: The effects of performance measurement on organizational identity in the social sector. *Entrepreneurship Theory and Practice*, 34(4), 763–783.

Groupe d'experts intergouvernemental sur l'évolution du climat (2022). Climate Change 2022: Impacts, adaptation and vulnerabilty: Summary for policymakers. Report.

Guibert, N. and Dupuy, Y. (1997). La complémentarité entre contrôle "formel" et contrôle "informel" : le cas de la relation client-fournisseur. *Comptabilité contrôle audit*, 3(1), 39–52.

Hamel, G. (2020). The quest for resilience. In *XXXI ISPIM Innovation Conference: Innovating in Times of Crisis*. ISPIM, July.

Hamel, G. and Pavillet, M.-F. (2012). *Ce qui compte vraiment. Les 5 défis pour l'entreprise : valeurs – innovation – adaptabilité – passion – idéologie*. Eyrolles, Paris.

Hasselbladh, H. and Kallinikos, J. (2000). The project of rationalization: A critique and reappraisal of neo-institutionalism in organization studies. *Organization Studies*, 21(4), 697–720.

Hatchuel, A. and Weil, B. (1999). *Pour une théorie unifiée de la conception, Axiomatiques et processus collectifs*. Presses des Mines/CNRS, Paris.

Haverman, H. (1993). Follow the leader: Mimetic isomorphism and entry into new markets. *Administrative Science Quarterly*, 38(4), 593–627.

Henri, J.-F. (2006). Management control systems and strategy: A resource-based perspective. *Accounting, Organizations and Society*, 31(6), 529–558.

Herman, R.D. and Renz, D.O. (1999). Theses on nonprofit organizational effectiveness. *Nonprofit and Voluntary Sector Quarterly*, 28(2), 107–126.

Hirst, G., Knippenberg, D.V., Chen, C., Sacramento, C.A. (2011). How does bureaucracy impact individual creativity? A cross-level investigation of team contextual influences on goal orientation–creativity relationships. *Academy of Management Journal*, 54(3), 624–641.

Hollandts, X. (2009). La gestion participative, une utopie réalisée ? *Revue internationale de l'économie sociale*, 313, 86–98.

Hood, C. (1991). A public management for all seasons? *Public Administration*, 69, 3–19.

Hopper, T. and Major, M. (2007). Extending institutional analysis through theoretical triangulation: Regulation and activity-based costing in Portuguese telecommunications. *European Accounting Review*, 16(1), 59–97.

Janssens, M. and Steyaert, C. (1999). Human and inhuman resource management: Saving the subject of HRM. *Organization*, 6(2), 181–198.

Johannessen, J., Olsen, B., Lumpkin, G.T. (2001). Innovation as newness: What is new, how new, and new to whom? *European Journal of Innovation Management*, 4(1), 20–31.

Jørgensen, B. and Messner, M. (2009). Management control in new product development: The dynamics of managing flexibility and efficiency. *Journal of Management Accounting Research*, 21(1), 99–124.

Kaplan, R.S. (2001). Strategic performance measurement and management in nonprofit organizations. *Nonprofit Management & Leadership*, 11(3), 305–360.

Kaplan, R.S. and Norton, D. (1992). The balanced scorecard: Measures that drive performance [Online]. Available at: http://www.hbs.edu/faculty/ Pages/item.aspx?num=9161.

Karasek, J. and Robert, A. (1979). Job demands, job decision latitude, and mental strain: Implications for job redesign. *Administrative Science Quarterly*, 24(2), 285–308.

Kline, S.J. and Rosenberg, N. (1986). An overview of innovation. In *The Positive Sum Strategy, Harnessing Technology for Economic Growth*, Landau, R. and Rosenberg, N. (eds). National Academy Press, Washington, DC.

Koenig, G. (2006). L'apprentissage organisationnel : repérage des lieux. *Revue française de gestion*, 160(1), 293–306.

Koestler, A. (1964). *Le cri d'Archimède*. Calmann-Lévy, Paris.

Lambert, C. and Sponem, S. (2009). La fonction contrôle de gestion : proposition d'une typologie. *Comptabilité contrôle audit*, 15(2), 113–144.

Latour, B. (1987). *Science in Action: How to Follow Scientists & Engineers Through Society*. Harvard University Press, Cambridge.

Latour, B. and Woolgar, S. (1979). *Laboratory Life: The Social Construction of Scientific Facts*. Sage, Los Angeles [Online]. Available at: http://www. bruno-latour.fr/fr/node/218.html.

Laville, J.-L. (2009). Management et régulation dans les associations. *Connexions*, 91(1), 149–161.

Laville, J.-L. and Glémain, P. (2009). *L'économie sociale et solidaire aux prises avec la gestion*. Desclée de Brouwer, Paris.

Le Goff, J.-P. (2003). *Les illusions du management : pour le retour du bon sens*. La Découverte, Paris.

Le Loarne, S. and Blanco, S. (2009). *Management de l'innovation*. Pearson France, Paris.

Lemaire, C. (2013). Le processus de construction d'un outil de contrôle de gestion inter-organisationnel. Le cas de l'expérimentation d'un outil de pilotage de la performance dans le secteur médico-social. PhD thesis, Université de Strasbourg [Online]. Available at: https://tel.archives-ouvertes.fr/tel-00919679.

Lenfle, S. and Loch, C. (2010). Lost roots: How project management came to emphasize control over flexibility and novelty. *California Management Review*, 53(1), 32–55.

Levinthal, D. and March, J.G. (1981). A model of adaptive organizational search. *Journal of Economic Behavior & Organization*, 2(4), 307–333.

Lieberman, M.B. and Asaba, S. (2006). Why do firms imitate each other? *Academy of Management Review*, 31(2), 366–385.

Light, P.C. (2000). *Making Nonprofits Work: A Report on the Tides of Nonprofit Management Reform*. Brookings Institution Press, Washington.

Lofsten, H. (2014). Information structures and business performance – Implications for technology-based firm's innovation performance. *Knowledge and Process Management*, 21(4), 246–259.

Löning, H., Mallerret, V., Méric, J., Pesqueux, Y. (2003). *Le contrôle de gestion. Organisation et mise en œuvre*, 3rd edition. Dunod, Paris [Online]. Available at: https://www.decitre.fr/livres/le-controle-de-gestion-9782100521678.html.

Lorino, P. (1995). *Comptes et récits de la performance*. Les Éditions d'Organisation, Paris.

Malcolm, D.G., Roseboom, J.H., Clark, C.E., Fazar, W. (1959). Application of a technique for research and development program evaluation. *Operations Research*, 7(5), 646–669.

Malmi, T. and Brown, D.A. (2008). Management control systems as a package: Opportunities, challenges and research directions. *Management Accounting Research*, 19(4), 287–300.

Mayer, J.C. (2016). Influencer l'attention des décideurs – Les pratiques d'"issue-selling" des risk managers. *Revue française de gestion*, 42(255), 75–88.

McKim, R.H. (1980). *Experiences in Visual Thinking*. Brooks/Cole, Boston.

Méda, D. (2000). *Qu'est-ce que la richesse ?* Flammarion, Paris.

Merchant, K. (1982). The control function of management. *Sloan Management Review*, 23(4), 43–55.

Merrien, F.X. (1999). La nouvelle gestion publique : un concept mythique. *Lien social et politiques*, 41, 95–103.

Meyer, M. and Ohana, M. (2007). Les entreprises sociales dans un monde marchand : à la recherche d'un management efficace des hommes. *Management & avenir*, 11(1), 187–202.

Meyer, J.W. and Rowan, B. (1977). Institutionalized organizations: Formal structure as myth and ceremony. *American Journal of Sociology*, 83(2), 340–363.

Meyssonnier, F. (2015). Quel contrôle de gestion pour les startups ? *Comptabilité contrôle audit*, 21(2), 33–61.

Midler, C. (1993). *L'auto qui n'existait pas : management des projets et transformation de l'entreprise*. Interéditions, Paris.

Mintzberg, H., Ahlstrand, B., Lampel, J. (2005). *Safari en pays stratégie : l'exploration des grands courants de la pensée stratégique*. Village mondial, Paris.

Moisdon, J.-C. (2005). Comment apprend-on par les outils de gestion ? Retour sur une doctrine d'usage. In *Entre connaissance et organisation : l'activité collective*, Lorino, P. (ed.). La Découverte, Paris [Online]. Available at: https://www.cairn.info/entre-connaissance-et-organisation-l-activite-coll–9782707145895-page-239.htm?contenu=resume.

Moquet, A.C. (2005). De l'intégration du développement durable dans la stratégie au pilotage et à l'instrumentation de la performance globale. *Management & avenir*, 3, 153–170.

Navarre, C. (1989). La nouvelle fonction project management. In *Communication au colloque "Réussissez votre gestion de projet"*. Institute for International Research, Paris.

Neukam, M. and Bollinger, S. (2022). Encouraging creative teams to integrate a sustainable approach to technology. *Journal of Business Research*, 150, 354–364.

Nixon, B. (1998). Research and development performance measurement: A case study. *Management Accounting Research*, 9(3), 329–355.

Nobre, T. and Zawadzki, C. (2013). Stratégie d'acteurs et processus d'introduction d'outils de contrôle de gestion en PME. *Comptabilité contrôle audit*, 19(1), 91–116.

Nonaka, I. and Takeuchi, H. (1995). *The Knowledge-Creating Company: How Japanese Companies Create the Dynamics of Innovation*. Oxford University Press, New York.

Nonaka, I., Byosiere, P., Borucki, C.C., Konno, N. (1994). Organizational knowledge creation theory: A first comprehensive test. *International Business Review*, 3(4), 337–351.

Obstfeld, D. (2012). Creative projects: A less routine approach toward getting new things done. *Organization Science*, 23(6), 1571–1592.

Ocasio, W. (1997). Towards an attention-based view of the firm. *Strategic Management Journal*, 18(1), 187–206.

Ocasio, W. (2011). Attention to attention. *Organization Science*, 22(5), 1286–1296.

OECD (2005). *Manuel d'Oslo : principes directeurs pour le recueil et l'interprétation des données sur l'innovation*. OECD, Paris.

Osborn, A.F. (1953). *Applied Imagination*. Scribner, Oxford.

Ouchi, W.G. (1979). A conceptual framework for the design of organizational control mechanisms. *Management Science*, 25(9), 833–848.

Parodi, M. (2004). Les valeurs, les principes et les règles de l'économie sociale traversent tous les domaines de la gouvernance et de la gestion. *Actualités Recma* [Online]. Available at: http://recma.org/actualite/les-valeurs-les-principes-et-les-regles-de-leconomie-sociale-traversent-tous-les-domaines.

Pearson, A.W. (1991). Managing innovation: An uncertainty reduction process. In *Managing Innovation*, Henry, J. and Walker, D. (eds). Sage, London.

Perray-Redslob, L. and Malaurent, J. (2015). Traduction d'un outil de contrôle de gestion dans le secteur public – Le cas du BSC dans l'armée de terre française. *Revue française de gestion*, 41(250), 49–64.

Plantz, M.C., Greenway, M.T., Hendricks, M. (1997). Outcome measurement: Showing results in the nonprofit sector. *New Directions for Evaluation*, 75, 15–30.

Porter, M. and Ketels, C. (2003). UK competitiveness: Moving to the next stage. *DTI Economics Paper*, 3(URN 03/988).

Raedersdorf Bollinger, S. (2015). Entreprendre dans l'économie sociale et solidaire : entre contrôle et créativité ? *Innovations*, 48(3), 69–85.

Raedersdorf Bollinger, S. (2018). La construction d'un outil de contrôle de gestion innovant dans l'économie sociale et solidaire : le cas de la fondation Apprentis d'Auteuil. *Innovations*, 57(3), 109–136.

Raedersdorf Bollinger, S. (2019). Creativity and forms of managerial control in innovation processes: Tools, viewpoints and practices. *European Journal of Innovation Management*, 23, 214–229 [Online]. Available at: https://www.emerald.com/insight/content/doi/10.1108/EJIM-07-2018-0153/full/html.

Retolaza, J.L., Aguado, R., San-Jose, L. (2020). Social accounting as an enabling tool to develop collective organizational citizenship behavior in the Diocese of Bilbao. *Frontiers in Psychology*, 11, 77.

Richez-Battesti, N., Petrella, F., Vallade, D. (2012). L'innovation sociale, une notion aux usages pluriels : quels enjeux et défis pour l'analyse ? *Innovations*, 38(2), 15–36.

Rousseau, F. (2007). L'organisation militante. *Revue internationale de l'économie sociale*, 303, 44–66.

Royer, I. and Zarlowski, P. (1999). Échantillon(s). In *Méthodes de recherche en management*, Thiétart, R.-A. (ed.). Dunod, Paris.

Rubin, H.J. and Rubin, I.S. (2005). *Qualitative Interviewing: The Art of Hearing Data*, 2nd edition. Sage, Thousand Oaks.

Salmon, C. (2008). *Storytelling*. La Découverte, Paris.

Schumpeter, J.A. (1911). *Théorie de l'évolution économique recherches sur le profit, le crédit, l'intérêt et le cycle de la conjoncture*. Dalloz, Paris.

Schumpeter, J.A. (1942). *Capitalisme, socialisme et démocratie*. Harper, New York.

Scott, W.R. (1994). Institutional analysis: Variance and process theory approaches. In *Institutional Environments and Organizations*, Scott, W.R. and Meyer, J.M. (eds). Sage, Thousand Oaks.

Scott, W.R. (2001). *Institutions and Organizations*, 2nd edition. Sage, Thousands Oaks.

Shalley, C.E., Zhou, J., Oldham, G.R. (2004). The effects of personal and contextual characteristics on creativity: Where should we go from here? *Journal of Management*, 30(6), 933–958.

Simons, R. (1987). Accounting control systems and business strategy: An empirical analysis. *Accounting, Organizations and Society*, 12(4), 357–374.

Simons, R. (1994). How new top managers use control systems as levers of strategic renewal. *Strategic Management Journal*, 15(3), 169–189.

Simons, R. (1995a). Control in an age of empowerment. *Harvard Business Review*, 73(2), 8–88.

Simons, R. (1995b). *Levers of Control: How Managers Use Innovative Control Systems to Drive Strategic Renewal*. Harvard Business School Press, Boston.

Spekle, R.F., Van Elten, H.J., Widener, S.K. (2017). Creativity and control: A paradox. Evidence from the levers of control framework. *Behavioral Research in Accounting*, 79(2), 73–96.

Suchman, M.C. (1995). Managing legitimacy: Strategic and institutional approaches. *The Academy of Management Review*, 20(3), 571–610.

Szostak, B., Yahiaoui, S., Seran, H., Lanciano, E. (2013). L'appropriation d'un outil de gestion issu du privé par des militants d'une organisation de l'ESS. Le cas de la boucle téléphonique au sein de la MAIF. In *Première journée de recherche international GESS*. Marne-la-Vallée.

Szostak, B.L., Boughzala, Y., Diné, S., Yahiaoui, S. (2018). La dynamique d'appropriation des outils de gestion dans le champ de l'ESS : est-elle spécifique ? *Management & avenir*, 100(2), 111–133.

Teller, R. (1999). *Le contrôle de gestion : pour un pilotage intégrant stratégie et finance*. Management et société, Paris.

Tidd, J., Bessant, J., Pavitt, K. (2006). *Management de l'innovation : intégration du changement technologique, commercial et organisationnel*. De Boeck, Louvain-la-Neuve.

Touchais, L. (2006). Le contrôle de gestion dans une dynamique de changement : définition d'un cadre d'analyse. *Comptabilité, contrôle, audit et institution(s)*, May.

Townley, B., Cooper, D.J., Oakes, L. (2003). Performance measures and the rationalization of organizations. *Organization Studies*, 24(7), 1045–1071.

Valéau, P. (2003). Différentes manières de gérer les associations. *Revue française de gestion*, 146(5), 9–22.

Van de Ven, A.H. (1986). Central problems in the management of innovation. *Management Science*, 32(5), 590–607.

Vatteville, É. (2006). Normes comptables et responsabilité sociale de l'entreprise. *Revue de l'organisation responsable*, 1(1), 30–37.

Von Krogh, G. and Grand, S. (2000). Justification in knowledge creation: Dominant logic in management discourses. In *Knowledge Creation: A Source of Value*, Von Krogh, G., Nonaka, I., Nishiguchi, T. (eds). St Martin's Press, New York.

Waggoner, D.B., Neely, A.D., Kennerley, M. (1999). The forces that shape organisational performance measurement systems: An interdisciplinary review. *International Journal of Production Economics*, 60, 53–60.

Wenger, E. (1999). *Communities of Practice: Learning, Meaning, and Identity*. Cambridge University Press.

Zaltman, G., Duncan, R., Holbeck, J. (1973). *Innovation and Organizations*. Wiley, New York.

Index

Other titles from

in

Innovation, Entrepreneurship and Management

2023

DARTIGUEPEYROU Carine, SALOFF-COSTE Michel
Futures: The Great Turn (Innovation and Technology Set – Volume 18)

PEYROUX Élisabeth, RAIMOND Christine, VIEL Vincent
Development and Territorial Restructuring in an Era of Global Change: Theories, Approaches and Future Research Perspectives

SAULAIS Pierre
Knowledge and Ideation: Inventive Knowledge Analysis for Ideation Stimulation (Innovation and Technology Set – Volume 17)

2022

AOUINAÏT Camille
Open Innovation Strategies (Smart Innovation Set – Volume 39)

BOUCHÉ Geneviève
Productive Economy, Contributory Economy: Governance Tools for the Third Millennium (Innovation and Technology Set – Volume 15)

ZAFEIRIS Konstantinos N, SKIADIS Christos H, DIMOTIKALIS Yannis, KARAGRIGORIOU Alex, KARAGRIGORIOU-VONTA Christina
Data Analysis and Related Applications 1: Computational, Algorithmic and Applied Economic Data Analysis (Big Data, Artificial Intelligence and Data Analysis Set – Volume 9)
Data Analysis and Related Applications 2: Multivariate, Health and Demographic Data Analysis (Big Data, Artificial Intelligence and Data Analysis Set – Volume 10)

2021

ARCADE Jacques
Strategic Engineering (Innovation and Technology Set – Volume 11)

BÉRANGER Jérôme, RIZOULIÈRES Roland
The Digital Revolution in Health (Health and Innovation Set – Volume 2)

BOBILLIER CHAUMON Marc-Eric
Digital Transformations in the Challenge of Activity and Work: Understanding and Supporting Technological Changes (Technological Changes and Human Resources Set – Volume 3)

BUCLET Nicolas
Territorial Ecology and Socio-ecological Transition (Smart Innovation Set – Volume 34)

DIMOTIKALIS Yannis, KARAGRIGORIOU Alex, PARPOULA Christina, SKIADIS Christos H
Applied Modeling Techniques and Data Analysis 1: Computational Data Analysis Methods and Tools (Big Data, Artificial Intelligence and Data Analysis Set - Volume 7)
Applied Modeling Techniques and Data Analysis 2: Financial, Demographic, Stochastic and Statistical Models and Methods (Big Data, Artificial Intelligence and Data Analysis Set – Volume 8)

DISPAS Christophe, KAYANAKIS Georges, SERVEL Nicolas, STRIUKOVA Ludmila
Innovation and Financial Markets (Innovation between Risk and Reward Set – Volume 7)

VALLIER Estelle
Innovation in Clusters: Science–Industry Relationships in the Face of Forced Advancement (Smart Innovation Set – Volume 36)

2020

ACH Yves-Alain, RMADI-SAÏD Sandra
Financial Information and Brand Value: Reflections, Challenges and Limitations

ANDREOSSO-O'CALLAGHAN Bernadette, DZEVER Sam, JAUSSAUD Jacques, TAYLOR Robert
Sustainable Development and Energy Transition in Europe and Asia (Innovation and Technology Set – Volume 9)

BEN SLIMANE Sonia, M'HENNI Hatem
Entrepreneurship and Development: Realities and Future Prospects (Smart Innovation Set – Volume 30)

CHOUTEAU Marianne, FOREST Joëlle, NGUYEN Céline
Innovation for Society: The P.S.I. Approach (Smart Innovation Set – Volume 28)

CORON Clotilde
Quantifying Human Resources: Uses and Analysis (Technological Changes and Human Resources Set – Volume 2)

CORON Clotilde, GILBERT Patrick
Technological Change (Technological Changes and Human Resources Set – Volume 1)

CERDIN Jean-Luc, PERETTI Jean-Marie
The Success of Apprenticeships: Views of Stakeholders on Training and Learning (Human Resources Management Set – Volume 3)

DELCHET-COCHET Karen
Circular Economy: From Waste Reduction to Value Creation (Economic Growth Set – Volume 2)

MEUNIER François-Xavier
Dual Innovation Systems: Concepts, Tools and Methods
(Smart Innovation Set – Volume 31)

MICHAUD Thomas
Science Fiction and Innovation Design (Innovation in Engineering and Technology Set – Volume 6)

MONINO Jean-Louis
Data Control: Major Challenge for the Digital Society
(Smart Innovation Set – Volume 29)

MORLAT Clément
Sustainable Productive System: Eco-development versus Sustainable Development (Smart Innovation Set – Volume 26)

SAULAIS Pierre, ERMINE Jean-Louis
Knowledge Management in Innovative Companies 2: Understanding and Deploying a KM Plan within a Learning Organization
(Smart Innovation Set – Volume 27)

2019

AMENDOLA Mario, GAFFARD Jean-Luc
Disorder and Public Concern Around Globalization

BARBAROUX Pierre
Disruptive Technology and Defence Innovation Ecosystems
(Innovation in Engineering and Technology Set – Volume 5)

DOU Henri, JUILLET Alain, CLERC Philippe
Strategic Intelligence for the Future 1: A New Strategic and Operational Approach
Strategic Intelligence for the Future 2: A New Information Function Approach

FRIKHA Azza
Measurement in Marketing: Operationalization of Latent Constructs

SKIADAS Christos H., BOZEMAN James R.
Data Analysis and Applications 1: Clustering and Regression, Modeling-estimating, Forecasting and Data Mining
(Big Data, Artificial Intelligence and Data Analysis Set – Volume 2)
Data Analysis and Applications 2: Utilization of Results in Europe and Other Topics
(Big Data, Artificial Intelligence and Data Analysis Set – Volume 3)

UZUNIDIS Dimitri
Systemic Innovation: Entrepreneurial Strategies and Market Dynamics

VIGEZZI Michel
World Industrialization: Shared Inventions, Competitive Innovations and Social Dynamics
(Smart Innovation Set – Volume 24)

2018

BURKHARDT Kirsten
Private Equity Firms: Their Role in the Formation of Strategic Alliances

CALLENS Stéphane
Creative Globalization
(Smart Innovation Set – Volume 16)

CASADELLA Vanessa
Innovation Systems in Emerging Economies: MINT – Mexico, Indonesia, Nigeria, Turkey
(Smart Innovation Set – Volume 18)

CHOUTEAU Marianne, FOREST Joëlle, NGUYEN Céline
Science, Technology and Innovation Culture
(Innovation in Engineering and Technology Set – Volume 3)

CORLOSQUET-HABART Marine, JANSSEN Jacques
Big Data for Insurance Companies
(Big Data, Artificial Intelligence and Data Analysis Set – Volume 1)

SAMIER Henri
Intuition, Creativity, Innovation

TEMPLE Ludovic, COMPAORÉ SAWADOGO Eveline M.F.W.
Innovation Processes in Agro-Ecological Transitions in Developing Countries
(Innovation in Engineering and Technology Set – Volume 2)

UZUNIDIS Dimitri
Collective Innovation Processes: Principles and Practices
(Innovation in Engineering and Technology Set – Volume 4)

VAN HOOREBEKE Delphine
The Management of Living Beings or Emo-management

2017

AÏT-EL-HADJ Smaïl
The Ongoing Technological System
(Smart Innovation Set – Volume 11)

BAUDRY Marc, DUMONT Béatrice
Patents: Prompting or Restricting Innovation?
(Smart Innovation Set – Volume 12)

BÉRARD Céline, TEYSSIER Christine
Risk Management: Lever for SME Development and Stakeholder Value Creation

CHALENÇON Ludivine
Location Strategies and Value Creation of International Mergers and Acquisitions

CHAUVEL Danièle, BORZILLO Stefano
The Innovative Company: An Ill-defined Object
(Innovation between Risk and Reward Set – Volume 1)

CORSI Patrick
Going Past Limits To Growth

D'ANDRIA Aude, GABARRET Inés
Building 21st Century Entrepreneurship
(Innovation and Technology Set – Volume 2)

DAIDJ Nabyla
Cooperation, Coopetition and Innovation
(Innovation and Technology Set – Volume 3)

FERNEZ-WALCH Sandrine
The Multiple Facets of Innovation Project Management
(Innovation between Risk and Reward Set – Volume 4)

FOREST Joëlle
Creative Rationality and Innovation
(Smart Innovation Set – Volume 14)

GUILHON Bernard
Innovation and Production Ecosystems
(Innovation between Risk and Reward Set – Volume 2)

HAMMOUDI Abdelhakim, DAIDJ Nabyla
Game Theory Approach to Managerial Strategies and Value Creation
(Diverse and Global Perspectives on Value Creation Set – Volume 3)

LALLEMENT Rémi
*Intellectual Property and Innovation Protection: New Practices
and New Policy Issues*
(Innovation between Risk and Reward Set – Volume 3)

LAPERCHE Blandine
Enterprise Knowledge Capital
(Smart Innovation Set – Volume 13)

LEBERT Didier, EL YOUNSI Hafida
International Specialization Dynamics
(Smart Innovation Set – Volume 9)

MAESSCHALCK Marc
Reflexive Governance for Research and Innovative Knowledge
(Responsible Research and Innovation Set – Volume 6)

MASSOTTE Pierre
*Ethics in Social Networking and Business 1: Theory, Practice
and Current Recommendations*
*Ethics in Social Networking and Business 2: The Future and
Changing Paradigms*

MASSOTTE Pierre, CORSI Patrick
Smart Decisions in Complex Systems

MEDINA Mercedes, HERRERO Mónica, URGELLÉS Alicia
*Current and Emerging Issues in the Audiovisual Industry
(Diverse and Global Perspectives on Value Creation Set – Volume 1)*

MICHAUD Thomas
*Innovation, Between Science and Science Fiction
(Smart Innovation Set – Volume 10)*

PELLÉ Sophie
*Business, Innovation and Responsibility
(Responsible Research and Innovation Set – Volume 7)*

SAVIGNAC Emmanuelle
The Gamification of Work: The Use of Games in the Workplace

SUGAHARA Satoshi, DAIDJ Nabyla, USHIO Sumitaka
*Value Creation in Management Accounting and Strategic Management:
An Integrated Approach
(Diverse and Global Perspectives on Value Creation Set –Volume 2)*

UZUNIDIS Dimitri, SAULAIS Pierre
*Innovation Engines: Entrepreneurs and Enterprises in a Turbulent World
(Innovation in Engineering and Technology Set – Volume 1)*

2016

BARBAROUX Pierre, ATTOUR Amel, SCHENK Eric
*Knowledge Management and Innovation
(Smart Innovation Set – Volume 6)*

BEN BOUHENI Faten, AMMI Chantal, LEVY Aldo
Banking Governance, Performance And Risk-Taking: Conventional Banks Vs Islamic Banks

BOUTILLIER Sophie, CARRÉ Denis, LEVRATTO Nadine
Entrepreneurial Ecosystems (Smart Innovation Set – Volume 2)

BOUTILLIER Sophie, UZUNIDIS Dimitri
The Entrepreneur (Smart Innovation Set – Volume 8)

BOUVARD Patricia, SUZANNE Hervé
Collective Intelligence Development in Business

GALLAUD Delphine, LAPERCHE Blandine
Circular Economy, Industrial Ecology and Short Supply Chains (Smart Innovation Set – Volume 4)

GUERRIER Claudine
Security and Privacy in the Digital Era (Innovation and Technology Set – Volume 1)

MEGHOUAR Hicham
Corporate Takeover Targets

MONINO Jean-Louis, SEDKAOUI Soraya
Big Data, Open Data and Data Development (Smart Innovation Set – Volume 3)

MOREL Laure, LE ROUX Serge
Fab Labs: Innovative User (Smart Innovation Set – Volume 5)

PICARD Fabienne, TANGUY Corinne
Innovations and Techno-ecological Transition (Smart Innovation Set – Volume 7)

2015

CASADELLA Vanessa, LIU Zeting, DIMITRI Uzunidis
Innovation Capabilities and Economic Development in Open Economies (Smart Innovation Set – Volume 1)

CORSI Patrick, MORIN Dominique
Sequencing Apple's DNA

CORSI Patrick, NEAU Erwan
Innovation Capability Maturity Model

FAIVRE-TAVIGNOT Bénédicte
Social Business and Base of the Pyramid

GODÉ Cécile
Team Coordination in Extreme Environments

MAILLARD Pierre
Competitive Quality and Innovation

MASSOTTE Pierre, CORSI Patrick
Operationalizing Sustainability

MASSOTTE Pierre, CORSI Patrick
Sustainability Calling

2014

DUBÉ Jean, LEGROS Diègo
Spatial Econometrics Using Microdata

LESCA Humbert, LESCA Nicolas
Strategic Decisions and Weak Signals

2013

HABART-CORLOSQUET Marine, JANSSEN Jacques, MANCA Raimondo
VaR Methodology for Non-Gaussian Finance

2012

DAL PONT Jean-Pierre
Process Engineering and Industrial Management

MAILLARD Pierre
Competitive Quality Strategies

POMEROL Jean-Charles
Decision-Making and Action

SZYLAR Christian
UCITS Handbook

2011

LESCA Nicolas
Environmental Scanning and Sustainable Development

LESCA Nicolas, LESCA Humbert
Weak Signals for Strategic Intelligence: Anticipation Tool for Managers

MERCIER-LAURENT Eunika
Innovation Ecosystems

2010

SZYLAR Christian
Risk Management under UCITS III/IV

2009

COHEN Corine
Business Intelligence

ZANINETTI Jean-Marc
Sustainable Development in the USA

2008

CORSI Patrick, DULIEU Mike
The Marketing of Technology Intensive Products and Services

DZEVER Sam, JAUSSAUD Jacques, ANDREOSSO Bernadette
Evolving Corporate Structures and Cultures in Asia: Impact of Globalization

2007

AMMI Chantal
Global Consumer Behavior

2006

BOUGHZALA Imed, ERMINE Jean-Louis
Trends in Enterprise Knowledge Management

CORSI Patrick *et al.*
Innovation Engineering: the Power of Intangible Networks

Printed and bound by CPI Group (UK) Ltd, Croydon, CR0 4YY

23/04/2025

14660910-0001